"Sergio Troncoso takes us on his journey ..., from child to husband, and student to father. He describes the solitary struggle of the writer, and the social and political hurdles overcome. Troncoso understands that in emerging from his chrysalis, he can never go back—nor does he want to. But the lesson is clear: You give something up to gain something else. As they say in the *mercado* in Chihuahua, 'What will you take for it?' Troncoso paid quite a lot, and it is worth our while to witness this journey from native son to the bloody birth of a public intellectual."

—Kathleen Alcalá, author of *The Desert Remembers My Name*

"Border-crossings is a metaphor for the experience of Hispanic-American professionals traversing America's 'borders' on their way to making a better life for self, family and country. Troncoso's use of short stories, as if entries in a personal diary, captures important life-impacting times along his journey from the barrio through elite higher education to a life as a caring father and husband even while continuing to navigate the nearly always invisible barriers of exclusion. Readers interested in modern day acculturation will want to read and reflect on this rare opportunity to crawl into the mind of a talented, Latino author who writes about a common Latino professional's story, and draw from his openness lessons intended to make us all better people."

—Frank Alvarez, President and CEO of the Hispanic Scholarship Fund

**Praise for the work of Sergio Troncoso:**

"Typical themes of love, death, coming-of-age and family life drive the narratives, but the El Paso setting lends them cultural depth. A series of tales about older men and women explores their vulnerability, loneliness and faith in God as they near death, while other stories concentrate on young adults caught in the cultural gap between their Mexican heritage and American lives. These stories are richly satisfying."

—*Publishers Weekly* on *The Last Tortillas and Other Stories*

"Single handedly redefines the Chicano novel and the literary thriller." —*The El Paso Times* on *The Nature of Truth*

# CROSSING BORDERS

## PERSONAL ESSAYS

SERGIO TRONCOSO

Arte Público Press
Houston, Texas

*Crossing Borders: Personal Essays* is funded in part by grants from the city of Houston through the Houston Arts Alliance.

*Recovering the past, creating the future*

Arte Público Press
University of Houston
452 Cullen Performance Hall
Houston, Texas 77204-2004

Cover design by James F. Brisson
Cover art by CiCi Segura Gonzalez

Troncoso, Sergio, 1961-
    Crossing Borders: Personal Essays / by Sergio Troncoso.
        p.   cm.
    ISBN 978-1-55885-710-0 (alk. paper)
        1. Troncoso, Sergio, 1961- 2. Troncoso, Sergio, 1961-
    —Family. 3. Authors, American—21st century—Biography.
    4. Mexican American authors—Biography. 5. Mexican Americans—Ethnic identity. 6. Interfaith marriage—United States.
    I. Title.
    PS3570.R5876Z46 2011
    818′.5403—dc23
                                                    2011025375
                                                        CIP

♾ The paper used in this publication meets the requirements of the American National Standard for Information Sciences—Permanence of Paper for Printed Library Materials, ANSI Z39.48-1984.

11 12 13 14 15 16 17          10 9 8 7 6 5 4 3 2 1

For Aaron and Isaac

# Acknowledgements

I WOULD LIKE TO THANK THE FOLLOWING PUBLICATIONS FOR first publishing my essays. "Fresh Challah" and "Crossing Borders" originally appeared in *Hadassah Magazine*; "Latinos Find an American on the Border of Acceptance" and "Terror and Humanity" appeared in *Newsday*; "The Father is in the Details" in the *Westchester Review*; "Apostate of my Literary Family" in *Pembroke Magazine*; "A Day Without Ideas" and "Trapped" in *T-Zero Quarterly*; "A Third Culture: Literature and Migration" in *Literal Magazine: Latin American Voices*; and "This Wicked Patch of Dust" in *The Packinghouse Review*. Blog entries from Chico Lingo have been reprinted in *Newspaper Tree* and *The News* from Mexico City.

# Table of Contents

# Crossing Borders

IN MY LIFE, I HAVE CROSSED MANY GEOGRAPHICAL, LINGUISTIC, cultural and even religious borders to the point where I often ask myself where do I belong, who am I really and who am I becoming.

I grew up dirt poor on the Mexican-American border of El Paso, Texas, and went to Harvard and Yale. Although I was raised a Catholic by my Mexican parents, I now attend services for High Holy Days on Manhattan's Upper West Side with my wife and two boys, Aaron and Isaac. Yes, I am a traveler between cultures and religions, but I do know who I am. The question that often burns in my mind, however, is why these border crossings are not attempted by more people. They should be.

I understand it is perilous to cross to the other side, whatever that "other" side is. You traverse into a no-man's land. You leave your "home" and possibly risk alienating those who stayed behind. I have been asked by many Latino writers and friends if I am now Jewish. I know often there is an undercur-

1

rent of surprise and even anger, at least by the most weak- or fearful-minded, when I proudly tell them about my wife, Laura, and my children. I was at a Latino book festival recently, at a restaurant with four writers. We were discussing the links and differences between Judaism and Christianity, a discussion I had prompted. I turned to a poet, who had been quiet for most of the evening, and pointed out that the artist on her T-shirt, Frida Kahlo, was half Jewish and half Mexican-Catholic. The poet, a proud Mexicana, seemed stunned at first, and then looked at her T-shirt as if she were looking at it for the first time. Yes, I said, we create pure beginnings to simplify things, maybe to build our self-esteem, but in reality we are interrelated, *mestizo*, in more ways than we can imagine.

The other peril to crossing borders is that you might not be accepted by your new family and friends. Laura and I met in college, and after seven years together, when we announced we were getting married, let us just say I did not get a heroic welcome at her parents' kitchen table. But I never gave up. Laura's aunts and uncles, brother and sister, took me in almost immediately. But I think it took another 10 years before Laura's father and especially her mother accepted me wholeheartedly. During that time, our two wonderful boys had been born, and we had survived a serious personal trial. In many ways, that horrible trial not only opened up old wounds, but also finally allowed them to heal forever. I was dedicated to Laura, and to our children. Laura's parents understood that is what mattered most of all.

In this personal history of crossing borders, I have often admired Ruth and her dedication to Naomi. Ruth, a Moabite, married Naomi's son, who soon died. When Naomi decided to return to Bethlehem, she urged Ruth to go back to her home and the gods of her people, but Ruth refused. "Do not ask me to leave you," Ruth said, "Wherever you go, I will go, and wherever you live, I will live. Your people will be my people, and your God will be my God. Only death will part us." Through hard work and perseverance, Ruth eventually found her place in a new land. The greatest king of the Israelites, David, came from a long line of ancestors beginning with Ruth. So, indeed, there are no pure beginnings, only survival, perseverance, dedication and reaching out to the "other" side.

# Literature and Migration

I GREW UP ON THE MEXICAN-AMERICAN BORDER OF EL PASO, Texas, about one kilometer from Mexico, the homeland of my parents who were from Chihuahua. In the barrio Ysleta, where I lived until high school, we spoke Spanish at home and on the streets, and English in school. I believed this bilingual border existence was not uncommon until I arrived at college. I was surprised to learn I suddenly had an accent and that not everyone was fluent in both Spanish and English. Mexican Americans were a miniscule minority in the Ivy League, yet in El Paso they had been the majority for most of the twentieth century.

What characterizes this migration from Spanish to English, from the culture of the Mexican-American border to the culture of the America's Northeast? The struggle for legitimacy was important. But I also became an outsider unwittingly, when I had not grown to consider myself an outsider in El Paso. Moreover, to jump from a proficient English to a literary English, I had to teach myself skills that perhaps were innate for many of my peers, skills that had been passed on to them by their parents. I had to teach myself on the fly, so to speak. Meanwhile, I struggled to fortify a sense of self that others saw as an exotic curiosity or an odd interloper.

In the beginning, the mantle of the outsider was thrust upon me by new surroundings. But later, I adopted the outsider status to communicate the good I saw in the Mexican-American community of El Paso to places like Harvard and Yale, Boston and New York. The first story I wrote, "The Abuelita," is about a Chicano who is a philosophy graduate student at Yale. Arturo phones his *abuelita* in El Paso to claw away at his loneliness, and ends up discussing Heidegger and his philosophy of death. The grandmother unintentionally gives him a response not just to his loneliness and being away from home, but also to Heidegger's philosophy, which values abstractions over the more quotidian concerns of the human being, like love and friendship. The honesty and character of the *abuelita* is pitted against the academic's pursuit of truth that too often overlooks the simplest, most humane solutions.

Again, when I wrote my first book, I donned the outsider status to try to communicate a world not well understood in the Northeast. In *The Last Tortilla and Other Stories*, I wrote philosophical stories about Chicanos to focus on their mental life, instead of on the physical, colorful traits I too often read in stereotypical American literature about Latinos. Also, I did not allow my publisher to italicize the Spanish whenever I used it, because in these border stories Spanish and English were often interchangeable, a unique hybrid language misunderstood not only by the purists in Washington, D.C. but also by those in Mexico City. A third culture, an in-between culture in which the antipodes matter less every day, is flourishing on the Mexican-American border.

My prose also tended to be simple and direct, another consequence of my migration from Spanish to English. I followed as my guide a favorite writer, Joseph Conrad, whose third or fourth language was English, yet who wrote searing literary works, including *Heart of Darkness*, which imprinted themselves into the souls of English readers. I didn't use words like "ideation," "deconstructing dynamics of power and authority" and "synthesizing structure." Perhaps when I was in New Haven as a graduate student in philosophy, I might have written like that, but I made it a point of eschewing such language forever. I still however use words like "eschewing." I can't help it.

Why did I write simply? When I started writing fiction, which was late in life for a writer, as a grad student, I wanted to get away from the meaningless abstractions of philosophical seminars. This linguistic pretension removed me from my community, from my father and mother, from my *abuelita*. For in classrooms within the Gothic fortress of Yale's Old Campus (and I suspect at many universities all over the world), a human being is first and foremost a mind. But in Ysleta, my home, the human being was, and is, feet. Feet in pain. Callused hands. Adobe houses built by those hands and feet. *La gente humilde* of Ysleta.

At Yale I was reacting against the elitism of the academy, an elitism that is hard to overcome when you can immerse yourself in books and forget the workers who make that world possible. I was also reacting against myself. I loved reading German and Greek philosophers. They did provide unique, unconventional insights into the human being. I had become an Ivy Leaguer in many ways. I was torn, between the people I loved at home and the ideas I devoured away from home.

I also noticed that many of the practitioners of academic fancy language, as I'll call it, were individuals who treated people poorly. Their education and facility with argument and power encouraged lying, deception and manipulation. The nature of truth, the pursuit of abstraction in universities, was a passive aggressive violence. Eliminate your opponent, not by killing him, but by warping arguments to win at any cost, by murdering his mind. The nature of truth was hate.

When you view human beings as abstractions, then it is easy to abuse those abstractions without guilt. Judging a person as a category is the root of racism; it is the root of cruelty. Moreover, writing about the world of people is an exercise in abstraction, and explains my deep ambivalence about being a writer. Too often my writer friends lose themselves in their world of words.

So I took a different tack with my literary fiction. I wanted to write so my father and mother could understand me. I was writing for them, and to give voice to those from Ysleta. I wrote simply. I also wrote prose obsessed with details, personal stories, to give meat to those understanding my community outside the American mainstream. I used myself as an example to provide a meaningful character struggling with complex issues, within the murk between right and wrong.

Yet I also wanted to explore ideas from Yale, and beyond, which I thought were worthwhile, so I wrote philosophical stories questioning the basis of morality. I wrote stories that asked whether murder was always wrong, or belief in God always holy, or success the root of moral failure. Most importantly, I believed the people of Ysleta had a lot to teach the people at Harvard and Yale about being good human beings. I still believe that.

But this effort to be clear and direct about difficult questions has sometimes condemned me in academic circles or among those who prize the beauty of language above all. I am also overlooked by those who never desire to think beyond the obvious and the popular. I write philosophical stories. You will never find my fiction at Wal-Mart or Costco.

I am in between. Trying to write to be understood by those who matter to me, yet also trying to push my mind with ideas beyond the everyday. It is another borderland I inhabit. Not quite here nor there. On good days I feel I am a bridge. On bad days I just feel alone.

From being a besieged outsider needing a voice, to becoming an outsider by choice deploying my voice (in English), the final significance of my cultural and linguistic migration has been philosophical. I like to ask difficult, often unpopular questions that get to the root of issues contemporary society ignores. Against much of popular American fiction, my stories are not primarily to entertain the reader, but to unmoor him. I want the reader to face through my characters perhaps what he will not face himself. In the United States, I ask: What is an American? How does abandoning or reforming your "home country" to join American culture affect your psyche, your sense of belonging, your relationships to neighbors who may be different from you? How do you build a community when you often don't have a common religion, race, ethnicity or even language? How do you build a sense of truth in this multicultural world? Is the United States still the promise land?

I think the role of a writer, not just a writer who is an immigrant in the culture in which he writes, should be to separate himself or herself from that society and culture, and be an outsider. Often the media are manipulated by those with money. The majority of citizens rarely bother to ask and try to answer tough questions, since they are immersed in making a living, the affairs of family and the immediate concerns of their personal lives. The average person, if he reads at all, will want to escape from local and national problems with a story that takes him somewhere else. The writer, I believe, should use this groundwork to his advantage. He should tell a good story, because without it you will never attract much attention nor have many readers. But any writer who is satisfied with only telling a good story is not living up to what great literature can be.

You must prod, and enlighten, and question the reader, then you must reveal through the particulars of character and plot and story what will stay with the reader long after he puts your book down. What he will gain is a seed of truth told through the experience of story, a seed that will grow in him, and thousands like him, and let him know first that he is not alone, and second that he can think differently than others, and third that he can act in small and important ways to reflect this new world in his life. We are all in some sense outside the world we inhabit. But a great story brings us together by linking the quiet thoughts of free and imaginative thinkers through time.

# Fresh Challah

AS SOON AS I WALKED INTO THE ROYALE BAKERY ON 72ND STREET
and Broadway, I knew I would get good Challah. The air was
heavy with the aroma of freshly baked bread. A worker in a
stained white apron marched with a metal sheet of braided
bread loaves gripped in his hands and held above his head.
With one swift motion, he slid the sheet onto the shelves
against the wall. The loaves of Challah glistened under the
bright white light, and seemed soft and steamy from the other
side of the cash register. Arrayed behind a glass counter were
vanilla crescents, lemon squares, *linzer törtchen*, dandies, hazelnut spirals, chocolate-dipped sables and *rugelach*. I was in
heaven, and I was not about to leave, so I slid into one of three
Formica booths against the wall. An old woman, not higher
than five feet, with a bouffant hairdo under a black hairnet,
her skin a creamy pallid except for the smear of rouge on her
cheeks, shuffled toward me. Her long, stiff apron seemed to
snag her legs, and I worried she would tumble forward at any
moment, but she did not. She asked me with a generous smile

and a wink if I wanted a cup of coffee. I said that I did and felt immediately guilty for having sat down to be waited on by somebody whose bluish hair reminded me of my grandmother. She did not seem to notice my discomfort and brought back my extra light coffee with, to my surprise, two pieces of *rugelach* on a paper plate. She winked at me again. I was really in heaven at the Royale.

Tomorrow would be Yom Kippur in Manhattan. I decided to fast from sunup to sundown and reflect on the number and variety of my wrongs over the past year and what I could do to correct them and why it had taken Yom Kippur to focus on my problems and resolve them. Maybe I would not even accomplish what might become clear in my head. Thinking rightly did not imply doing the right thing. Aristotle had argued that point against Plato, and I knew it only too well. Yet as I relaxed at the Royale Bakery and stared at the customers waiting at the counter, sipping my coffee which slithered down my throat like a hot snake, I hoped that whatever failings I uncovered in my character, whatever festering wounds I found in my soul, could be changed, or at least better understood. I rarely had melodramatic crises. I mostly endured self-imposed irritations that coalesced into questions refusing to leave me and bedeviling my mind.

As I chewed on a raisin of the *rugelach*, I thought about one question that had perplexed me for months. I was not Jewish, but in some sense wanted to be. True, the woman I loved was Jewish. But that did not explain how I felt. I also loved *rugelach*, Challah, *kasha* knishes, Passover *tsimmes* and matzoh ball soup, my favorite. Yet I would also travel many miles for white-meat mole *poblano*, deep-fried *carnitas* from a Juárez bistro, my mother's fresh flour tortillas and succulent, tangy *asaderos* from Licon's Dairy in Clint, Texas. It was invariably true that my religious and cultural epiphanies contained a culinary *sine qua non*. I often became a believer in a cause or a country through my stomach.

But in what other sense did I want to be Jewish? I could only explain that feeling by describing how I wanted to be Mexican like my grandmother, Doña Dolores Rivero. Whenever I looked at my *abuelita*, I wanted so much to protect her. Even if her dark brown eyes were downcast and weary, she was poised for a fight. I wanted to ensure she did not have a hard life anymore; I wanted her to enjoy an elusive peace in her soul. Most of all, I wanted her steely optimism never to be crushed by evil. She had always been tough, and she also knew how to hurt her toughest grandchild, the one with such a sharp tongue. So we understood each other only too well.

My *abuelita* often told me about her life as a child on a Chihuahua ranch, yet I could tell she often kept many things from me. She spoke of her childhood as if a type of pain was too vivid to explain with mere words and too personal to confess to someone you loved. So the stories she recounted were always haunted with what was not said. Around every dark turn in her stories, I could palpably sense how lucky she felt to have survived. Maybe she believed the explicit details of her history would expose her as something less than human. Maybe she thought she had lived a life so painful from where she was now in El Paso, on her shady porch drenched with sunlight on Olive Street, that it was better to keep those ghosts in the past. Perhaps Doña Dolores did not want to reveal how human beings could be so cruel to each other, and so she would keep her grandchild hopeful.

This was what I knew of my grandmother's life, from her stories to what my parents and their friends had said about Doña Dolores Rivero. She had grown up poor in rural northern Mexico during the social chaos of the Mexican Revolution. Several uncles and brothers perished in a civil war in which over a million Mexicans died. Those who survived were refugees for years, with little food, dying of disease, alone to fend for themselves and without any real local authority to protect them. I had the suspicion that my grandmother might have been raped when government soldiers and gangs of armed horsemen swept through small hamlets scattered across the Chihuahua plains. No one in my family would utter the word "rape," although my *abuelita* said in a whisper that no law existed in the middle of the desert with a war raging behind every hill and valley. I did know my grandmother had in fact shot men with a rifle, and maybe that was the truth: she had shot and killed the men who had wanted to abuse her. I knew that as a child my *abuelita* had defended her mother from being beaten by her husband, and placed herself between her parents.

As a young girl, Doña Dolores had been known for her strength. Not only was she tough-minded, but she was also physically tough. She could sling a 50-kilo sack of beans over her shoulders and toss it into the back of a grain truck. I knew working men would be embarrassed to be near her, because she was often stronger than they were. I also knew my *abuelita* possessed a sympathetic heart, perhaps a bit too vulnerable for her own good. She fell deeply in love with a man who is hardly spoken of in my family. She had three children by him, but he never married my grandmother. She alone raised two daughters and a son in the Chihuahua desert. My mother told me she did not own a single pair of shoes until she was a teenager. I was also told that many men, seeing my grandmother with children but not married, assumed they could have their way with her, that she was available for the taking. Bad assumption. That was when my grandmother learned to shoot a rifle.

When Doña Dolores was older, in her forties, she met the man I would know as my grandfather. Don José Rivero was a good man, quick with a smile, loyal and tolerant of my headstrong grandmother. I loved my grandmother (and, of course, my grandfather), yet I knew she was difficult to live with. Perhaps this was due to the many deep scars from her life ("Dolores," in Spanish, means sorrows), or perhaps she already possessed that incredible will that was ready to die rather than be defeated. In any case, she would do what she wanted to do, or else. Doña Dolores ran her household with an indomitable spirit. My mother and her siblings were put to work to pay the bills. My grandfather handed over his check to my grandmother, although I also knew he secretly stashed a few dollars for his small pleasures, beer and cigarettes.

Yet my *abuelita* was also loving and needful. She would stack the record player with her albums of polkas and *corridos* —her favorites were from Los Coyotes del Río Bravo—and twirl my rickety grandfather around the living room on an afternoon so hot you thought your skin would melt. When I saw them dance in their apartment in El Paso's Segundo Barrio, I often wondered if this was how they met, since my grandfather had played a silver-and-black accordion with a *norteño* band.

My *abuelita's* home, in front of a red-brick halfway house run by the Catholic Church, was often full of *viejitos* on a Saturday night. All sorts of characters came over to see her and sit on her porch and smoke cigarettes. They would talk about God. They would laugh until the desert night became too cold. They would ask her for advice on their problems and rediscover the laughter that kept them happy and alive. I loved those nights. I was the only child among them, and I remember hearing about a great faith in God and about what was important in life and what did not matter. I remember my *abuelita* saying to keep fighting for what was right and never give up on life even if others despoiled it. When Doña Dolores died a few months after my grandfather's own death, I felt alone in the world for the first time. But then I remembered what she had said and what she had done, and I resolved to fight for what was right, to seek a critical faith and to defend others who had the courage to better themselves.

In my grandmother, I saw someone with a great spirit to live. She was a person who found meaning in life despite, and because of, her pain. Of course, my *abuelita* did not desire her trials, but her character survived and surmounted her bleak history. By meeting the tribulations of history with flinty courage and skill, she created her destiny. Doña Dolores possessed a character that pushed her forward to willing what she thought was right. It was never an easy road, yet her willfulness was a method of illuminating her self. That Live-Free-Or-Die attitude guaranteed Doña Dolores would face many obstacles and naysayers. Many thought my *abuelita*, with one lazy eye askew and the other glaring at you, was just stubborn beyond belief.

But those who confronted my grandmother misunderstood her and misunderstood being willfully right. Many of my grandmother's challengers simply did not like the idea of a willful woman. Other Mexican machos were accustomed to getting their way, and when they fought with Dolores Rivero the exchange was a violent clash of wills. But my grandmother was more than just willful. When a bully wanted to abuse another victim, my grandmother would defend the weak. When a man puffed himself up at another's expense, my grandmother deflated the braggart. She was not just contrary. She tried to be right.

How did Doña Dolores determine what was right in her own mind? She began with self-worth. She always reminded me, in her warbled, adamant voice, that you could never achieve self-worth by putting others down. I saw that she achieved it by respecting herself, by struggling to improve her behavior and by criticizing her faults. That clear-eyed self-reflection was her way of developing standards for her willfulness. My *abuelita* believed in God and tested her good actions everyday. In this manner, she gained a sense of what was possible, what was stupid, what was unjust, what was a real achievement and what was a waste of time. Yes, my *abuelita* was willful, but she also fought to understand what was right. My grandmother never confused her sense of righteousness with selfishness. She did not try to dominate an individual even if she could. Rather, her unflinching self-reflection engendered a simultaneously fearless and a vulnerable self. If Doña Dolores was familiar with her demons, if she conquered them, then she expected others to do the same. She would repeatedly give herself up, to trust again. She would offer a helping hand to a stranger at her screen door. She would say what everyone had been avoiding at a family dinner. Over the phone, she challenged me to conquer my fears at Harvard, a school with but a handful of Chicanos, in the distant and forbidding cold of New England. Or she might empathize and laugh with me at a disaster. I remember not only that strength of will, but also her hard-edged kindness. After Doña Dolores picked you up from a ruinous fall, she pushed you to get going again. The great fighters, she said, became great by what they did after being knocked down.

That vulnerable self-confidence my grandmother possessed was sometimes fraught with danger. When she criticized herself, she was harsh and even self-destructive. When my *abuelita* offered somebody a second chance, she left herself open to disappointment, or worse. Yet she always believed a person could rise from his miseries if he was willing to be honest about his problems. Opportunistic strangers took advantage of my grandmother, but at least they never did it for very long. I knew her trust had been shattered a few times, yet I never saw her retrench into hate. I never understood where she could find that reservoir from which to gather the strength to deliver herself to kindness again. But I believed she knew that if she did not open herself to new disappointments, she would also never trust anyone again. She refused to allow the ignoble world to win the war inside of her.

When I said I wanted to be Jewish, this was what I meant. In the Jewish community, I often found those who reminded me of my grandmother. I wanted to defend them from evil in the world, because I could see myself as that kind of person. I wanted to help good people who opened themselves to push beyond where they were, who had the character to overcome discrimination and alienation; I wanted these people to win in the world. In that sense, I wanted to be Jewish and I wanted to be Mexican.

I knew that in many respects I could never really be Jewish. My mother was not Jewish. I had not converted to the Jewish faith. Even if I had, I would probably never understand what it meant to be Jewish. How could a non-Jew ever comprehend 5,000 years of history and culture? The struggle against countless oppressors? Or the hermeneutics of the Torah? So there existed many ways in which I could never be Jewish. I imagined all the disparate strands of my life might come together one day if it were discovered that my ancestors were Spanish Jews expelled during the Spanish Inquisition to Mexico in the New World. I did not research this possibility, but maybe I should. (Recently, an engineer whose last name is also Troncoso sent me a research paper which described his work in Galicia, Spain, and neighboring Portugal, at the Castle of Trancoso. His conclusions? Trancoso and Troncoso were the same name, in different languages. More surprisingly, he found that "Troncoso" originated from the Ladino dialect and that the surname was Sephardic Jewish, as recorded in the census records of the Catholic Church in Spain. Troncoso was the name of one of many Jewish families banished to the New World in 1492.)

I also knew that not all Jews were Jewish in the sense I described, nor were all Mexicans like my grandmother. Many did not struggle against oppressors and against themselves, with a character that would not give up to defeat but that, instead, chiseled their form of human progress with self-respect and self-criticism. Maybe what I was thinking about was not ultimately Jewish or Mexican at all but, somehow, deeply human. I knew this humanity was not a niceness that the word nowadays connoted. The humanity I described was not blind acceptance of whatever was done. My humanity was hard-edged. It was a challenge to better yourself by making yourself vulnerable, to engage in making standards by asking yourself difficult questions. It was an exhortation to defend others in their quest for self-determination, because you grasped why life should be this way.

You gained respect for life by knowing what was possible when you were truthful and critical toward yourself. Nothing was long hidden from you. You knew exactly your good and evil. You nurtured the courage and stamina to keep improving yourself the more you lived such a vibrant life. I believed you finally developed the character to live with yourself, but this was anything but a complacent acceptance of who you were and what you did. Living with yourself created a gauntlet in front of you, because only that could truly respect life.

The best I could do now, after many years away from home, was to remember my *abuelita* Doña Dolores and what she taught me. I could struggle hard just as she did. I could remember how the heart of life was this struggle. When I brought home friends from the other side of the world, I could remember how this poor Mexican woman quickly identified with them after a few hours of coffee and conversation. It was as if these young strangers were also her grandsons and grand-daughters coming home. Years after they had met her, my friends had not forgotten this grandmother in the desert who had so quickly and sympathetically reached the core of who they were.

The old woman at the Royale Bakery finally returned with a round raisin Challah enough for six and a fresh plain Challah smaller than the first. She had convinced me to take the second one so that I could eat it before dinner. I also bought one half pound of *rugelach*, although after she dropped extra pieces into the box for free I had almost three quarters of a pound. She asked me if I lived on Manhattan's Upper Westside, and I said that I did, about ten blocks away. She told me she was happy to see the new faces at the Royale particularly during the high holy days. Then the place would bustle quite unlike the rest of the year. She appreciated the regulars who stopped in for their Challah every Friday. Yet she eagerly awaited the new, unfamiliar faces. Then she knew the high holy days were near and she would soon see her grandchildren.

# Letter to my Young Sons: Part One

TWO WEEKS AGO, AARON AND ISAAC, I LEARNED YOUR MOTHER Laura has breast cancer. My heart feels impaled. These words, so useless and feeble. Laura is only thirty-five years old. Her next birthday will be in only three days. I write this letter to you, my sons, with the hope that one day in the future you will read it and understand what happened to our family.

Together, your mother and I have created and nurtured an unbreakable bond that has transformed us into an unlikely team. A Chicano from El Paso, Texas. A Jew from Concord, Massachusetts. I want you to know your mother. She has given me hope when I have felt none; she has offered me kindness when I have been consumed by bitterness. I believe I have taught her how to be tough and savvy and how to achieve what you want around obstacles and naysayers.

Our hope is that the therapies we are discussing with her doctors will defeat her cancer. But a great and ominous void has suddenly engulfed us at the beginning of our life as a family. This void suffocates me. A few days ago, we relished chasing you, Aaron, brandishing your sword and shield. We delighted in beholding Isaac's waddle-run in the living room as you yelped your first words. Now, your mother and I play with both of you and encourage your antics, but inside, our souls are shattered. We have to struggle to overcome this airless and frightful void. We have to fight this tragic sense that our time is at a premature end. The writing helps me make sense of this awful news. Words slow it down to what I might control with my imagination. These sentences keep me from a scary free-fall into the chaos of mortality. This writing is my tool in our fight and a retreat from our nightmare. I pit these words against merciless breast cancer, prayers against infiltrating ductal carcinoma. Our gauntlet is our only hope: lumpectomy, mastectomy, chemotherapy, radiation. We must fight this fight together. Yet I still yearn for today to be in a providential future.

Not long ago Laura discovered a lump under her right breast. She has regularly inspected her breasts, because her mother had breast cancer and a mastectomy. After we returned from December vacations to El Paso, Texas, and Sanibel, Florida, Laura was reluctant to see her doctor. Perhaps she wanted to avoid the problem and wish it away. A few years back at a New York hospital, Laura had had an ovarian cyst removed. I remembered the fear I had fought as I waited for the preliminary pathology report while Laura recovered from anesthesia. An old, red-headed surgeon had called Laura's name and reported to me the ovarian cyst benign. I had been elated. Perhaps this was why Laura did not immediately call her doctor after our vacation: she expected another benign cyst. But by February I was angry at Laura for not scheduling the appointment. Laura met with her doctor, but his mammogram revealed a "suspicious anomaly." He referred her to a surgeon for a biopsy.

What you hope for is often not what happens. This time I waited in the day surgery area of another New York hospital. I still worried, yet I also hoped we would be lucky and the lump would only be a nuisance. A doctor called Laura's name and I walked up to him. He guided me to an area away from the room full of families, in the hallway. The suspicious anomaly, he said, was malignant. The surgeon added technical detail about adjacent tissue which also appeared pre-cancerous. I clumsily blurted out a few questions, and he indicated Laura would probably need a mastectomy. Later they would know more details.

I listened and nodded to a battery of appointments with specialists on different floors, another appointment to review the pathology report, procedures, the sequence of events and the words "malignant," "mastectomy" and "cancer" palpitating in the air like concussion bombs. The blood drained away from my face. I leaned against the wall to keep from collapsing onto the white linoleum floor. Time was yanked from its fast clip and compressed second by second to an incessantly heavy stop.

Laura and I had just stepped into a nightmare. She did not yet know it. She was still asleep. I did not panic, but felt a sense of suffocation, as if a thick sheet of black plastic had been wrapped tightly around my face. As soon as Laura awoke, the surgeon would speak to her and give her the news. I wanted to rush to her and hold her hand, but I could not. In the meantime, I phoned her parents in Concord, but nobody answered. I dialed my parents, and after my mother said hello it took every ounce of composure not to cry. The words were shards of glass in my throat. My parents were in disbelief. My mother soon sobbed and said she would spend the day praying at Mount Carmel in Ysleta.

I marched to the surgeon's office on another floor and made an appointment to review the pathology report in two days. I also scheduled an appointment with an oncologist recommended by the surgeon's staff. I wanted to attack the cancer immediately, anything but to wait or waste time shuttling between doctors' offices. I was desperate to see Laura. I returned to the recovery room, and the nurse said Laura would be ready in a few minutes. I found Laura hunched over in a dressing room no bigger than a closet. Laura is slight, with a small waist and big hips I have always adored. She has short, curly brown hair, and a face pallid and kind, with big blue eyes that are extremely near-sighted. In the dressing room, Laura wore her thick glasses and was crying. I hugged her and whispered I loved her and said we would fight this fight together. Her despair shoved me beyond my own anguish. How could we climb out of this void if we were both collapsed at the bottom?

At no other time have I wanted more to console Laura, to brush away her tears and to whisk her to a place better than the here and now. We trembled inside that tiny room. My heart heaved in spasms. Our reality crumbled around us, and beyond the destruction lay a dark silence. I took Laura home. The sunlight splashed on the sidewalk, but the light was harsh and vacant.

We waited a weekend until we received the pathology report. In the meantime, we frantically read different books on breast cancer. But the more I read, the more depressed I became. Breast cancer is an unrelenting disease. The danger is that it does not affect only the breast, but often escapes to other parts of the body. If breast cancer cells reach the liver, the patient will probably die within months. Lumpectomies, mastectomies and radiation are site-specific remedies. Only chemotherapy and hormonal therapy are systematic treatments for the entire body, but even they do not specifically target breast cancer cells. Rather, these therapies indiscriminately "carpet bomb" with the hope of also destroying unde-tected cancerous cells. We still did not know much about how to fight cancer. I reassured Laura I would love her even if a mastectomy was the best option. Her body is not who she is. Laura and I do love each other passionately, and one day I will write the story of how we met at a Mexico seminar at Harvard. I thought she was English and she thought I was Greek. Our love has never been confined to this earth. I love Laura's spir-it; I love how sweet she is when I am full of vinegar. I admire her kindness and devotion to our family. When I say I love her, I mean I love every bit of her, how she thinks, how she looks, the way she sacrifices for others, her vulnerabilities and triumphs, her generosity. After seven years of marriage, we shared a great love affair.

But the more I studied the research, the more I understood we would be lucky if a mastectomy definitively stopped the march of her cancer. Truly there would be no "end" at all. Just higher probabilities of survival with chemotherapy. A future so uncertain it was a nauseous free-fall. In one tumultuous day, we had lost our firm footing. What shattered was the belief in the quotidian fantasy that you will wake up tomorrow and it will be like today, and today will be like yesterday, for years to come. We rarely jump outside this groundwork fantasy, because most of us do not suffer life-threatening diseases until our old age. By then, we have had the benefit of time and the experience of our steadily declining bodies, and we can recog-nize the inevitable price to pay for our mortal voyage. We can have time to craft an edgy truce reconciling what we did with what we did not do. We can witness the marriage of our chil-dren and revel in our grandchildren. We can hope for their future, even as we see our end. When we fully appreciate that it is our fantasy that life is forever, then in our old age we might discover a quiet satisfaction with our lot. The whole of life. Laura and I only wanted more time. On Monday, we would find out more.

The pathology report was not good news. The surgeon reviewed the report paragraph by paragraph, explaining each technical term. I had written a list of questions from books that explained breast cancer pathology reports. First, the surgeon had found two tumors on her right breast, tumors not connected to each other. That in itself suggested Laura's cancer was aggressive. One of the tumors was four centimeters long, large for a tumor. Second, her nuclear grade was high, which meant that the rate at which cancer cells were dividing was fast. I hoped the pathologist had overestimated the nuclear grade. I clung to any hope. Third, her margins were positive. That meant the cancer was not confining itself where it began, but was spreading to adjacent breast tissue. Again, I had read the measurement of margins was imprecise. But how many times can you wish for lucky mistakes, when instead you should be facing the truth? Every detail of the report closed another exit from our claustrophobic nightmare. The surgeon had also detected necrosis and lymphatic invasion. Necrosis, or dead cancer cells, means the cancer has exhausted its initial blood supply and is expanding to other areas. Lymphatic invasion suggests that a cancer is potentially more dangerous than one without it.

Blow after blow after blow. I do not know how we withstood the barrage. The doctor repeated a modified radical mastectomy was certainly the right surgical response. That, and chemotherapy we should discuss with our medical oncologist. Gross tests were still necessary, like a CAT scan and a bone scan, to determine if large bits of cancer were detectable anywhere else inside Laura's body. These tests would be immediately ordered by the surgeon's office. Laura questioned the doctor, and the middle-aged surgeon was patient, authoritative and somber. He showed us an Internet site to research articles on breast cancer, nutrition and new therapies. The doctor had never been pessimistic, yet he also had never said, as Laura pointed out later, that the pathology report contained any good news. We scheduled appointments for the gross tests, received extra copies of the pathology report and stepped out of his office. We sat down at a diner on First Avenue, our hands clasped together, and we were devastated.

For the first time, we discussed what I would do if the worst were to happen. The verb "discuss" fails to capture what transpired that afternoon at the diner in Manhattan. In that booth, we felt trapped on a ship plunging between gigantic waves. Our heads throbbed. The air itself betrayed us. Simple and kind words escaped from our lips, but fear crept in between us like a malevolent fog. Laura and I conversed quietly, but we were anything but calm. We both cried. We believed even a mastectomy would not be enough to stop the cancer. We believed Laura's cancer was particularly ferocious. We were certain we had been naïve about not facing the darkest voyage ahead.

After the lumpectomy, we had ignored the news and hoped for the best. But the day of the pathology report, we sunk into pitiless realities and the most gut-wrenching nightmares. We did not know our odds, but imagined a bleak future. Maybe we were right; maybe not. In five days, we would visit an oncologist who would explain our choices and give us more information. Would Laura die in five years? Could chemo destroy all her cancerous cells? How would I take care of our two boys? That swirling void around us—disastrous news, sketchy facts, our ignorance, waiting for days, our greatest of fears—nearly swallowed us whole. We pulled each other from that black vortex, and sunk again under its brutal power. In desperation, we each reached for the other's outstretched hand.

I visited a church for the first time in years. I needed to pull Laura up from the abyss and to pull myself up too. I admit, it is hypocritical to ask God for help when your life unravels.

But I had never quarreled with God; I had never condemned Him in any way. The organized Church, preoccupied with materialism, entrenched in misogynous traditions? That was another story. I sat alone in church three times the week we learned the results in the pathology report. It is a modest Catholic church on 82nd Street, near Broadway. During the day, it was silent and empty. When I approached the wooden pews for the first time, I felt like a hypocrite. I thought about leaving immediately like an intruder, but then I slipped into a pew, weary of carrying my body, and made my peace with God. I told Him about Laura.

The next day I returned and I did not care anymore about my past conflicts with the Church. I did not care about my hypocrisy. I did not care whether God would be angry with me for seeking Him now, in my desperation. I only wanted Laura to be healthy. I wanted Him to help her, so I prayed. I gave myself up and begged for help. If He was real, I needed His power more than ever. I sobbed and asked for help in a way I have never asked for anything else in my life. The pews and alcoves were shadowy dark. Alone, I think I understood how completely I loved Laura and how I yearned for her to be with us for a long time. You forget these truths when your life is a series of frantic mornings and achy evenings. What is essential is lost in the everyday.

The first week after we spoke with the breast surgeon was terrifying. No one yet was in charge of Laura's treatment. We were consumed by dread, our greatest fears encircling us like phantoms. Laura's father, who is a neurologist, had helped us find an oncologist at Memorial Sloan-Kettering, where we believed Laura would receive the best cancer treatment in New York. But we had to wait another week for that appointment. In the meantime, we met with a plastic surgeon recommended by the breast surgeon who had originally performed the lumpectomy. This meeting calmed both of us, although plastic surgery, if Laura chose it, would only be the cosmetic part of her treatment. As the plastic surgeon reassured us, we were able to glimpse at the other side of our dark landscape, recovery and survival. Laura was not sure about breast reconstruction. What we appreciated, after questioning the plastic surgeon and reading about plastic surgery for breast cancer patients, was that Laura might gain psychological benefits if she awoke after her mastectomy with a new breast. Her operation would be longer, her recovery more arduous, with reconstruction than without.

Most young women with breast cancer opt for reconstruction. I am certain some elect this choice because of sheer vanity. Beyond vanity, there also exists a sense of wanting to create a distance between you as a patient and you as a survivor. That psychological distance will help a person function and even thrive years later. In a patient's mind, she may suspect that cancer cells may still be floating inside her body, that recurrence is an ever-present possibility. But before any concrete news, she may discover an elusive peace, and that peace will be key for survival. Patients with a positive, or at least a neutral, attitude are often healthier years later, in comparison to similarly diagnosed patients who are uniformly pessimistic about their chances.

With the plastic surgeon, Laura and I discussed what procedure Laura might want. An implant, a TRAM flap or a TRAM flap with microsurgery (sometimes called a "free flap"). Laura did most of the talking, and I asked a few questions. One of the doctor's patients happened to be in the waiting room. The doctor opened an examination room, and the young woman, also a cancer patient, was nice enough to show Laura the results. For the first time in a long time, Laura smiled.

We also scheduled a CAT scan and a bone scan. The main problem with breast cancer is that it can spread to the rest of the body. A patient's immune system will attack stray cancer cells. But a virulent form of cancer may spread anyway. Too many cancer cells can overwhelm a body's ability to kill them. Gross tests allow the doctors to detect large chunks of cancer in the body. A patient's chances of survival are much lower if her CAT scan or bone scan reveals the spread (or metastasis) of her breast cancer. Even if those scans are negative, microscopic bits of cancer may still be somewhere besides the breast. Chemo will have to defeat that invisible threat.

We waited in the radiology department for Laura's turn. First, she had a CAT scan, which lasted forty-five minutes. I tried to lose myself by reading the newspaper, but nothing in *The New York Times* mattered to me anymore. I wanted only to will a good result into reality. I wanted to send Laura any positive energy to help her. But I was truly helpless. Laura returned and sat down, and she was handed a radiological milkshake before the bone scan. That elixir would highlight any anomalies in her bones. A young radiologist soon reported that the CAT scan appeared "perfectly normal," and we were thrilled. This was the first piece of good news since the pathology report.

I told Laura I wanted to call her mother. I wanted everyone to know Laura's CAT scan was negative. Maybe we could start hoping for a good overall result. Maybe we might yet climb out of this wretched black void and be free again. We waited more than an hour for the results of the bone scan. Again the test was negative, and Laura and I were relieved. Yet in my mind—maybe sensing irrationally that the more I allowed myself to hope, the harsher the eventual truth would be—I began to worry these were preliminary conclusions. A staff radiologist had interpreted these scans, not an expert on breast cancer, bone cancer or lung cancer. Others would also study these films, and maybe they would uncover something new. Just as we regained the blessed normality we had taken for granted, I did not want to tempt the bad luck demons to pounce on us later.

That week I also told Aaron's teachers about our news. The Bank Street School for Children is such a wondrous place for a kid. I have always admired the attention and care the teachers bestow upon their students. I have learned how to be a better father from studying these interactions. I love my boys more than these inert words can ever symbolize. But at times I know I can be gruff and irascible. I am impatient. The thoughts in my head often burst through my mouth like a fusillade. When I am exhausted with dozens of near-emergencies fresh in my mind, I allow my worst instincts to prevail. I do not always succumb to that tension, but once in a while I will yell in exasperation, particularly after another sleepless night. I want to quash that bad self when it beckons. I am not too proud to admit I have made a mistake, and apologize. As a father, my goal has been to travel the hard road from the crutch of apology to changing my character permanently, so that I do not repeat my mistakes.

I appreciate individuals who possess the patience and understanding I strive to achieve. I admire good teachers, and Bank Street is a training ground and a haven for master teachers. When I told Aaron's teachers about Laura, my favorite, the one who seemed delighted to see my child every morning, cried silently. As I whispered to the teachers about our nightmare, three boys climbed a "space ship" on its way to the moon. A four-year-old girl with blond curls dipped her fingers in white "slime" and traced wide circles on a tray. A mom read *Peter Pan* to her son in the reading nook, and he squealed as she lowered her voice for the tick-tock crocodile. I thought my head would explode with my private anguish. I told the teachers I would keep them informed, and one suggested visiting the school psychologist. Later the psychologist would have good ideas about how to talk to Aaron about Laura's illness.

At the end of that first week, Laura and I told Aaron the news. We wanted to be the ones to tell him; we wanted to keep our three-year-old hopeful and exuberant. We worried about what to say and how to anticipate his questions. We expected him to ask if his "Mamá Linda" would die. Two months earlier, the movie The Lion King had prompted Aaron to ask me what happened when somebody died. In the story, Mufasa dies, and poor Simba is left fatherless and believes he is responsible for his father's death. Later, the young lion can talk to his father, who appears in the sky to remind him of his heritage. Aaron asked me if we would all die, and if one day he would die too. With tears in his eyes as we tucked him into bed, Aaron said he did not want to die and leave "home." He wanted to stay with us for a long time, and he did not want us to leave home either. That night we talked to Aaron before he settled down. I assured him he could stay with us for as long as he wanted. I told him he would always sleep in his bed, with baby Isaac next to him. For as long as he wanted, he could stay in his room and we would always be next door. Aaron lay his head on the pillow and wiggled under the covers. Before I left his room, Aaron asked me to "check" him five times that night. I said that I would.

Now, instead of explaining death in a Disney movie, Laura and I talked to Aaron about her cancer. We told him the doctors had discovered a lump in Mom and were removing it to make her better. We said the lump was called cancer, although as the psychologist had earlier predicted that word did not mean much to Aaron. Mom would get better, we said, but she would have to stay in the hospital for five days when the doctors removed the lump. We also mentioned that after she returned home Mamá Linda would take more medicine (chemotherapy), and the medicine could make her throw up. Again, the psychologist had suggested mentioning chemo, because kids often expected their mothers to be fine after the hospital stay. Children might become fearful if they saw their mothers weary and nauseous from the toxic chemicals of chemotherapy. Children might also think these side effects were part of the illness. Aaron listened carefully, his dark brown eyes alert, with an attention span greater than any three-year-old I knew. He asked what a "lump" was. Laura explained it as best she could. Later when Laura underwent her mastectomy and breast reconstruction, that lump would cease to be an abstraction and become menacingly real. During her hospital stay, Laura would be away from the children for the longest time ever. Aaron's questions and fears would pour out daily. Isaac had not yet reached his first birthday.

Before the first week ended, we also sent the reports, tests and tissue slides to Memorial Sloan-Kettering. On Monday, we wanted to be ready when we met with Laura's new oncologist. The original breast surgeon scheduled Laura's surgery for the following week, with the plastic surgeon. But we knew the medical oncologist at Memorial would want the surgery and plastic surgery performed in-house. Different doctors we knew, including Laura's father and his colleagues, said Memorial was the best place for breast cancer care in New York. We scheduled those outside appointments anyway, which we later cancelled, because doing nothing was distressing.

When someone you love has breast cancer, you cannot wait and waste days waiting for something to happen. You want to act immediately against the disease to recapture a sense of control, which drains away from your life with every fact, fear and nightmare. Switching to Memorial meant that, once we met with Dr. Theodoulou, she would have to set up new appointments with a breast surgeon and plastic surgeon. Again we would have to wait. Those would be more days to give the cancer a chance to grow and spread inside Laura's body. What was the right thing to do in this madness? What if we did not like Dr. Theodoulou? The oncologist was the main person we would see for years, the one who might guide us out of this oppressive landscape. We would depend on her to help Laura live a long and blissful life. Yet we had not even met Maria Theodoulou. In this chaos, the choices and hopes we clung to seemed surreal.

Laura had a lumpectomy and biopsy on March 12th, and on Monday, March 23rd we met with Dr. Theodoulou. She had been recommended by a doctor friend of Laura's father. I discovered she was Greek (a member of the Hellenic Society of New York) and principal investigator of the HER 2 trial at Memorial Sloan-Kettering. HER 2, a receptor protein, is often present and "overexpressed" in women with breast cancer, which means that those receptors aid cancer cell growth. If a doctor can find antibodies that hinder HER 2, then she might slow down or stabilize the disease, especially if it has metastasized to other parts of the patient's body.

Dr. Theodoulou swept into her office like a gust of wind from the East River. She is energetic, aggressive, empathetic, smiley and blunt. I liked her immediately. If someone could help us in an intelligent and confident manner, then this doctor certainly would. Laura liked Dr. Theodoulou too. The doctor interviewed Laura for a while, asking her questions about her medical history and the findings of the first breast surgeon. Theodoulou said her lab had already conducted its own pathology report, and confirmed the details of the first report. Laura's breast cancer was an aggressive kind, and Theodoulou agreed a modified radical mastectomy was the right choice. She peered at the CAT scan which we brought with us, and concluded it looked normal. The doctor also wanted to inspect the bone scan immediately, and I promised to deliver it to her that day. The radiology department at the first hospital had asked for a few minutes to prepare the bone scan, but if we had waited we would have been late for our meeting with Dr. Theodoulou.

She also encouraged Laura to get tested for the genetic mutations (BRCA-1 and BRCA-2) often present in Jewish women of European descent, since Laura's mother had also been diagnosed with breast cancer. Laura's cancer, Dr. Theodoulou added, was highly estrogen positive, which meant it might be treatable with hormonal therapies like Tamoxifen. This fact as well as Laura's family history suggested that Laura should consider removing her ovaries. We were already blessed with two beautiful boys and we began to think seriously about this choice. Removing her ovaries would propel Laura into menopause, reduce her estrogen level and perhaps hinder the cancer's growth. Chemotherapy might accomplish the same goal, but over a period of several months.

Before we left her office, Dr. Theodoulou arranged appointments for Laura with the chief breast surgeon at Memorial Sloan-Kettering and the chief gynecologist. Theodoulou had apparently noticed another cyst in Laura's right ovary and wanted the gynecologist's opinion about it and removing the ovaries. Watching Theodoulou work, we had a sense that a bright, aggressive doctor was finally in charge of Laura's treatments. Laura returned to work at Chase—where her colleagues to her boss to her boss's boss had been supportive—and I walked from Theodoulou's office to our first hospital to retrieve the bone scan.

I brought the film back to Memorial, and walked directly into Theodoulou's office. The doctor waved me in and was on the phone with Laura, who was already at Chase. Before Laura hung up, Theodoulou looked at the film as I waited for her response. It wasn't a good one. Dr. Theodoulou detected a "shadow" in Laura's sternum and wanted Laura to return the next day for an X-ray. The doctor did not conclude, as did the first radiologist, that the scan was "perfectly normal." I walked out of that office feeling alone. I wanted to hold Laura's hand. I knew at that moment she also felt alone. You think you clear a hazard, you receive "good news," and suddenly it is not good news at all. The floor trembles and cracks open at your feet, and you lose your footing again and drop into a world of terror. How had this damn "shadow" been missed the first time around? Had breast cancer spread to Laura's sternum? What had Theodoulou found? She had assured me it was just a precaution, but this was what other doctors had said when they first wanted to perform a biopsy on the lump in Laura's right breast eleven days ago. These precautions were often the precursors of more disastrous news. My head throbbed as I searched for a bus that might return me to the Upper Westside. I tried to call Laura at work, but I could not find a street phone.

Although we reminded each other that Theodoulou was only being cautious about the shadow in the sternum, Laura and I were depressed that night. We wanted to hope, although we knew in our hearts we could be fooling ourselves. We could be denying what lay in front of our eyes. We did not know what news the next day would bring. We knew the odds of long-term survival were dismal if the breast cancer had spread. It was a dreadful night.

Before Laura's appointment, I returned to church and prayed for a good result. I had lost my inhibitions about asking God for help; I cared only about Laura and my two boys. Finally I understood a part of the meaning of God: to be selfless, to believe in a complete love of others, to give yourself up to a greater power and hope. Laura asked me not to accompany her to the X-ray; I had been to every doctor's appointment. Laura said I wasn't doing my work, which was true. It was only an X-ray that would take a few minutes. But she did want me to meet the new breast surgeon and gynecologist in a few days.

I did my best to return to my routine and finish writing projects I had started before the lumpectomy. Throughout that day, only one thought mattered to me: I wanted a good X-ray. Laura returned later that evening, and still we had no news about the X-ray and Theodoulou's conclusions. At forty-five minutes before midnight, the phone rang. Theodoulou told Laura that the X-ray did not show anything abnormal in the sternum and that the shadow in the bone scan was perhaps arthritis. The doctor apologized for calling so late—Laura and I were indeed already in bed, the lights off—but Theodoulou imagined we wanted the good news as soon as possible. She was right. We turned off the lights again. In the darkness, I inhaled for what seemed the first time that day.

One week after we met Theodoulou, we met with Patrick Borgen, the chief breast surgeon at Memorial, David Hidalgo, the chief plastic surgeon and Richard Barakat, the chief gynecologist. With Theodoulou we discussed what we wanted to do and why. After questioning the doctors, Laura and I were certain these were capable and careful professionals at the top of their fields. We believed we were in good hands. One of the problems of acquiring such medical firepower, however, is coordinating the doctors' schedules for your surgery. The first free date for all three doctors was Monday, April 13th, a week longer than we wanted to wait, but we took it. The mastectomy and removal of the ovaries would last forty-five minutes each, and the breast reconstruction about six hours. The plastic surgeon needed the entire day free of any scheduling conflicts to complete his work.

The doctors said the ovary removal would work well with the TRAM flap procedure, because the plastic surgeon could proceed from the abdominal opening made by the gynecologist to remove the ovaries. The TRAM flap consists of a tissue transfer which removes excess skin and shifts fat from the lower abdomen to the chest area, a tummy tuck in exchange for a new breast. One abdominal muscle remains attached to the fat tissue so the new breast can keep its blood supply. The new breast, as Laura's skin and blood, would be sensitive to touch. After the plastic surgery, Laura would have some abdominal weakness, because one of her two abdominal muscles would no longer function. Yet her normal activities, like picking up the boys, would not be compromised. Had she been an aerobic instructor, for example, she might not have wanted that procedure.

A TRAM flap with microsurgery ("free flap"), an option Laura did not choose, does not sacrifice one abdominal muscle completely. Only part of the abdominal muscle is removed in a free flap, and is reattached with microsurgery in the appropriate area. But with a free flap, there exists a small risk that the microsurgery will not take and the patient can potentially lose the tissue shifted from her abdomen. The TRAM flap with microsurgery is recommended only for those with a compelling reason to constantly use their abdominal muscles.

The week before April 13th, Laura donated blood for her surgery, and so did I. I felt pleased I could contribute to the success of Laura's surgery. I was also delighted Laura and I were the same blood type. We have been soul mates for years, and secretly I believed this confirmed it. Laura's brother and sister visited from Boston and also wanted to donate blood for Laura, but ironically, they were not her blood type. A Chicano from the desert and mountains of Francisco Villa and Pascual Orozco. A Jew from the woods of Ralph Waldo Emerson and Henry David Thoreau. Perhaps after being in love for many years, Laura and I had melded into one being, one force, one blood.

# Letter to my Young Sons: Part Two

LAURA'S DAY FOR SURGERY HAD ARRIVED, MONDAY, APRIL 13TH. Laura had been instructed to be at the hospital, across Central Park at York Avenue and 67th Street, at 7 a.m. We left our apartment on the Upper Westside when Broadway was still dark, the street empty. Our Guatemalan babysitter, Amparo Saenz, had commuted from Jamaica, Queens at an even earlier hour, to take care of Aaron and Isaac on this emotional, eventful day. Since this Monday was not a school day for Aaron, Amparo did not have the extra duty of taking both children on the bus to Bank Street.

As we drove in the taxi through the murky streets, Laura did not say anything until we entered the canyon of glittery mica walls under a canopy of trees in Central Park. "I'm a little scared," she whispered. I told her I would be in the hospital all day, until she exited surgery and the anesthesia recovery room. Later that day, her parents would be flying into New York from Boston. Laura and I knew this day would be the beginning of our fight against her breast cancer, and we were relieved the day had arrived. It had been dreadful to wait for appointments, and wait for test results, and wait again for Laura's date with surgery. We were not in control of our destiny. With every delay, we imagined we allowed Laura's cancer to act against her body until it might gain an insurmountable, deadly advantage. This day, April 13th, would be the longest day of my life.

At Memorial, we walked into the business office first, as we had been instructed. We filled out papers detailing our medical insurance, who would be responsible for bills not covered by insurance, home addresses, driver's license numbers. We were handed more papers and given directions where to report inside Memorial. Laura and I next sat in a white room, with beds on wheels, where nurses began to prep Laura for surgery. Doctors, or their assistants, would march into the room, ask Laura a few questions, obtain written authorizations for what they were about to do and leave. Dr. Hidalgo arrived and began to mark Laura's chest and abdomen with what looked like a Magic Marker: the location of his incisions, where he wanted the breast surgeon to conserve skin, the exact position of her ribs before the TRAM flap and the rearrangement of muscle and fat for the breast reconstruction. In a few moments, I thought, Laura had metamorphosed from a worldly New Yorker on Broadway, to a patient at a hospital, to a billing number, to a body, and these transformations occurred as if we were watching someone else on the silver screen.

Dr. Hidalgo had a soft, focused demeanor. I could barely hear him whenever he spoke, yet I had the sense he possessed great knowledge about his work. When Laura and I had waited in Hidalgo's Upper Eastside office, I had marveled at the oil paintings of yellow roses and white lilies by the doctor's hand: he was a man obsessed with the exquisite details of beauty. Dr. Borgen, the breast surgeon, had also been attentive and careful, but he was a general ready to command his soldiers through the most difficult terrain. Borgen was direct and forceful. His mind and his hands acted in concert. Whatever was in his mind was translated immediately to movement and action. Laura's surgery would have three parts. Borgen would perform the mastectomy on her right breast, and preserve much of the skin. He would also remove lymph nodes from under Laura's right arm to test them for cancer. If the lymph nodes tested positive, then the cancer had most likely spread beyond Laura's breast. Any discovery of the cancer's metastasis dramatically lessened Laura's chances for survival. After Borgen completed his work, Barakat and Hidalgo would work together. Hidalgo would make incisions in Laura's abdomen for the tissue that would be shifted to her reconstructed breast. Barakat, the gynecologist, would proceed further from these incisions and remove her ovaries. Borgen and Barakat would need about an hour each to finish their procedures, and Hidalgo would require six hours to reconstruct the breast.

One doctor after another. Good doctors. Maybe great doctors. But each performing major surgery on Laura. I knew she was brave. I prayed each procedure would unfold smoothly. I prayed the immense strain of this marathon surgery would not overwhelm Laura. I prayed the doctors would find nothing new. From experience, I knew that whatever the doctors could find with tests and X-rays could be vastly different from what they might discover with their eyes and hands. I did not want to cry, but I knew we faced many dangers on this fateful day. We needed effort and luck. We needed hope on our side.

A nurse marched into the prep room and said it was time to go. I accompanied Laura, who was strapped onto a stretcher, to the pre-operating room, where after a few minutes I would have to say goodbye. I carried a blue duffel bag with Laura's clothes: her jeans, blue cotton oxford shirt, which reminded me of El Paso, her bra, sneakers, white socks, earrings, Swatch, Hawaiian robe (a memento from our honeymoon) and blue slippers. As I followed the two attendants wheeling Laura down the hallway and into a huge elevator, my heart throbbed, but I smiled and rubbed her smooth, pale forehead. I would stay at Memorial, I repeated, until her surgery was over. I would not leave the hospital until I saw her again.

We arrived in the pre-op room with four stretchers with patients already waiting in between sky-blue curtains. As soon as Laura was settled into her spot and the pre-op nurse walked away, I kissed Laura and rubbed her cheek. I wanted to present a brave face to her, to give her all the *ánimo* I could muster, but inside I was terrified. I did not want this to be the last time I saw Laura. For a few seconds, she cried softly, her big blue eyes swimming in tears, and I reassured her she had excellent doctors who would take care of her. She told me one of her greatest fears was not having her glasses. Whenever Laura takes out her contact lenses, she wears thick Mr. Magoo glasses. The last time at Memorial, for the ovarian cyst she had removed years ago, Laura had handed her glasses to a nurse who had difficulty locating them after the operation. On this day, the pre-op nurse again informed Laura she could not wear her glasses in the operating room. Before I left I took them with me. As soon as the doctors allowed me to visit her in the post-anesthesia recovery room, I would bring Laura "her eyes."

I kissed Laura again, and the nurse returned and said the doctors were ready. Laura would be the first in line. I waved goodbye, and Laura was wheeled behind beige, metallic double doors. I imagined I would be beside her; I imagined I would magically transport myself next to her; I imagined I could guide the doctors' hands to be delicate, precise and true. I looked up and did not know exactly where I was. I spent the next half hour searching for the exit in a labyrinth of identical hospital corridors.

At the Memorial Sloan-Kettering waiting room, I slumped into a U-shaped black sofa-chair that enveloped me like a giant hand. I had waited in this room before, with a wall-to-wall picture window overlooking the trees and traffic of York Avenue. When Laura's ovarian cyst had been removed years ago, I had waited in this room for hours, until the old red-headed doctor had called Laura's name and reported to me the cyst benign. Now, the waiting room seemed smaller than I remembered, as if I had returned to my grade school classroom as an adult. In a way this was true. Our current ordeal was more serious than anything we had faced before. In between, we had reveled in joyous years and endured difficult ones, catapulting us into life as it is, life without illusions, our adult life.

The waiting room was busy, with people streaming in or out of several unmarked doorways, two escalators humming with a low drone, the gift shop glass doors swinging open and close, a wide hallway next to eight or ten elevators crowded with doctors, patients, nurses and visitors, and another narrower hallway to the cafeteria. It was hard to think of yourself as being alone in this room, and maybe that was the point. Yet, I was truly alone. I was alone next to families who also waited for any news, which too often was a vague, indecipherable medical jumble that did everything but release you from your anguish. I brought *The Wall Street Journal* and *The New York Times*, a book of short stories and work to edit, but I could not read any of it. To focus, I needed to pretend I was anywhere but Memorial Sloan-Kettering. To read, I needed to think of words as meaningful ciphers. But I could not accomplish that self-delusion. Who cared what words meant? I could only imagine what was happening to Laura. I wanted this day to be a good day for her.

When you wait in this room, hour after hour, an update nurse becomes your best friend. You wait your turn as she does her rounds throughout the room every two or three hours. Every word she utters you decode in your mind. Her responsibility is to inform family members, one family at a time, how

their beloved is progressing in the operating room, when the
doctors might be finished with surgery, when the family can
visit the patient in the recovery room. This nurse is your link
to your loved one. She will also warn you when the doctors
might call the phone at the information desk, or come down
in person, to offer you their conclusions, to ask you to make
crucial decisions on behalf of the patient.

I introduced myself to the update nurse the first time she
approached me. The nurse glanced at her list of patients for
that day. She had our home number and for some reason a
note indicating I would be at home waiting for news. She was
glad I had introduced myself, because otherwise she would not
have looked for me.

After the nurse left to talk to a Dominican family a few
empty seats away from me, I sat and prayed the breast surgeon
would find all the lymph nodes negative. That was the next
important threshold for Laura. Of course, even if a surgeon
found the lymph nodes negative, there could still be a chance
the cancer had spread beyond the breast to other parts of her
body. But the chances of her cancer being confined to the
breast were greater if the nodes were negative. I also worried
about Laura's stamina during this grueling day. She would
have to endure surgery for more than eight hours, under general anesthesia, multiple procedures performed on her body.
Would Laura be able to tolerate such trauma? She was young
and athletic, the reasons why her doctors had recommended
performing these three procedures consecutively. Yet even in
the hands of the most careful and skillful physicians, anything
could happen.

I glanced at passersby, as if staring at embodied seconds
striding before me. I stared at the face of a clock on the wall.
I wanted to escape to a place outside my head, beyond my
imagination, which dwelled on a disastrous turn of events. I
wanted the world of objects to counter my mind. These

objects outside my head would save me for one more moment or two. These human beings as objects, safely beyond my mind, would remind me of a life free of my turmoil. For hour upon hour, I fought my scary thoughts. I told the person at the information booth I would be in the cafeteria; I needed to get away from the waiting room for a few minutes. I needed to get away from myself. I gulped a cup of coffee and waited for the next update on Laura, in two hours.

Laura's parents arrived from Boston a few minutes past noon. I hugged my mother-in-law and shook hands with my father-in-law, and relayed what I knew so far. I get along with my in-laws okay. To tell you the truth, at times I believe I even love them. Yet the road to this crumbly emotional peak has been treacherous. We both love Laura, and this has always kept us together. I love my children and they love their grand-children. But when Laura and I dated—for seven years, through college and in graduate school, with Mexico City in between—my in-laws only tolerated me. I knew they secretly hoped I would go away. They did not like me because I was not Jewish; my mother-in-law said that to my face. I was also not docile and pliant. My favorite flag from the American Revo-lution, with a snake coiled and ready to strike, is emblazoned with the words "Don't Tread On Me." That's my motto. I sim-ply want to be left alone. But I think my in-laws expected a son-in-law to be like an obedient child. That is, they assumed they knew best and that they could tell me what to do, and that I would either do it or that at least I would not respond, without prettifying it, that I did not think such-and-such was a good idea. I believe in a live-and-let-live philosophy. Med-dle in my affairs, and expect a shove to the chest.

Over time I have forged an adult relationship with my par-ents, not only by demanding respectful treatment, but also by taking responsibility for my decisions. Also, my parents pushed their children out of the house, not because they did not love us, but because they did. Laura's parents were, and are, good parents. Yet they often included themselves in many decisions made by their children, with and without invitation. I often clashed with my in-laws, particularly during the initial years of our marriage, but I also tried to get along. Years would go by during which our relationship was amicable. Yet on a moment's notice, we could provoke each other into a bitter conflict.

Before Laura was diagnosed with breast cancer, we visited her parents in Massachusetts every other month. We spent one week of our Christmas-Hanukah vacation with them. After many years, I think my in-laws accepted me simply because I did not leave, and they realized their daughter loved me. On this day, in Memorial Sloan-Kettering's waiting room, we thought about the same things: that our beloved Laura would get well, that the doctors would find nothing in her lymph nodes, that now, more than ever, we needed to stick together as a family.

At a few minutes before four o'clock, the update nurse informed us that Borgen had completed the mastectomy, that Barakat had successfully removed the ovaries and that Hidalgo had begun the breast reconstruction. We had not yet heard from the doctors themselves. I remembered, as I had waited for news about Laura's ovarian cyst a few years ago, that a red-headed doctor had told me the cyst was benign in person. But on this day, I had seen more families called on the phone at the information desk than doctors in white smocks speaking to fathers, mothers, sisters and husbands. I wondered if this was another personalized service slipping into the past.

Laura's name was announced over the intercom. I rushed to the information desk, picked up the phone and heard a man who identified himself as Dr. Barakat, the gynecologist. Laura's father was standing next to me. Barakat said the ovary removal had been successful and that a small cyst they had detected prior to the operation had tested negative for cancer.

Everything else in Laura's ovaries was normal too. I was thrilled. Then Barakat handed the phone to Dr. Borgen, and the breast surgeon said the news could not have been better. None of the thirty lymph nodes Borgen had removed seemed positive from the pathologies they could perform immediately. None was enlarged. A shock of emotion stunned me, and I felt propelled into the air. Borgen said his doctors would study the lymph nodes more closely over the next few days, but he repeated that the news was excellent. I asked the doctors to repeat their news to Laura's father, who is a neurologist. He asked a few medical questions and was also pleased with the report. (I also figured, if Laura's doctors knew her father was a prominent doctor scrutinizing their every move, then these doctors might burn extra brain cells for Laura. I may not know about medicine, but I am an expert in politics.) Laura's father and I relayed the news to her mother, and together we were ecstatic. We could exhale. Our nightmare might soon end, and we could focus again on the little problems of life. I had yearned for a culmination to this day, but only one that might be a happy escape from our black void. This day, April 13th, was Passover, and my father-in-law and I left the waiting room to eat a late lunch, walking briskly to dispel our nervous elation. We munched on matzoh tuna sandwiches at a deli on First Avenue. I noticed the splash of sunshine against the brownstone façades. In New York City, it was the beginning of a resplendent spring.

We returned and waited for Hidalgo to finish the breast reconstruction. At a few minutes before 6 p.m., Hidalgo informed us the reconstruction had proceeded as expected. Laura was resting in the recovery room. His only concern was a small patch of skin where the blood circulation was not yet optimal. Yet he was confident that this minor problem would clear up in a few days. Hidalgo's staff would keep an eye on it.

Laura would stay in the post-anesthesia room for two hours, and we could see her before they wheeled her to her room on the tenth floor.

After I hung up the phone, I knew I was running out of time. If I could not see Laura soon, I would have to wait until morning. Amparo was home with the kids, and I knew she had a long subway ride from Manhattan to Queens. She had arrived at our apartment at six in the morning, and I would need her help the next day. I phoned Amparo and told her the good news about Laura. Amparo assured me she could stay as long as I needed her. At 8 p.m., the hospital staff said we could see Laura. Her father and I pushed open the double doors of the post-anesthesia recovery room, and we found Laura asleep on one of the beds against the wall.

Laura looked whiter than I have ever seen her. Her face was drawn, her eyes shut. Her neck revealed the dried-up splash of an amber liquid. I stroked her brown hair and repeated the good news. I was not sure she could yet hear me. Her father fiddled with her IV and asked the nurse to adjust it because the pain relief medication was not flowing properly. As my father-in-law reviewed the notes in a black binder left on Laura's stretcher, he was slightly reprimanded by another nurse. We repeated the news to Laura, and slowly she opened her blue eyes. We repeated what Borgen had told us: the lymph nodes were negative. I remembered the exhausted, yet happy smile of her sticky lips, her eyes half-closed, her throat swallowing hard, amber and white.

I asked her how she was feeling as I adjusted her oxygen mask. She mumbled a few words, "Not great . . . glad it's over . . . tired." I placed the glasses over her eyes. Laura wearily opened and closed them and smiled weakly. She drifted in and out of sleep. After a few minutes, she opened her eyes and said she was happy about the nodes. We watched her as she went back to sleep. Laura rhythmically exhaled and inhaled, each breath like a spectacular, slow-motion leap beyond an ocean. I told her I would be back in the morning and that her clothes were already in a locker in her room on the tenth floor. I thought she had not heard me, but without opening her eyes, she said, "Give Aaron and Isaac hugs and kisses from me."

I said goodbye to Laura's parents, who were staying in a hotel near the hospital. I rode the sluggish cross-town bus home. I was exhausted when I saw my two boys, but their embraces revived me. Amparo returned to Jamaica, Queens, and I read each boy a story before putting them to bed. Isaac has always been a good sleeper and closed his eyes as soon as he was in his crib. Aaron asked me about Mamá Linda, and I told him she was in the hospital and would be home soon. Tomorrow, I said, he could write her a letter and I would deliver it.

Memorial does not permit children to visit breast cancer patients on the tenth floor, because children may bring more germs from the outside. Laura would not be able to see Aaron and Isaac during her nine-day stay in the hospital, the longest time she had ever been away from them. The next day Aaron dictated to me the first of many letters to Laura. He promised to give her chocolates when she returned home. A few days later, three-year-old Aaron also talked to her on the phone, and held the phone to Isaac's ear so the baby could also hear Laura's voice. Laura wrote short notes, which I read to the kids every morning. I told them what their mother ate, how I needed their help to sneak in M & M's into the hospital. Aaron drew pictures of spaceships and animals and portraits of our family for Laura, Isaac colorful lightning bolts across the blank page, which she kept on her nightstand. Isaac's first birthday would be in three days. I thought about buying balloons and a cake for a small celebration.

The day after Laura's surgery, I woke up at 5 a.m. to take care of the boys before I returned to the hospital. I love Aaron and Isaac. Each day I relish being their father. I have also learned to be a better person because of my sons and what they have taught me: patience, wonder and curiosity. That morning I felt I could lift mountains. I knew I had to be out of bed and in the shower before Isaac awoke. I had already accomplished this hectic routine whenever Laura had traveled for two or three days for work. I brought the baby monitor into the bathroom so I could hear the boys in case they woke up. I showered and shaved quickly, every minute another task accomplished, one step closer to being on top of details rather than overwhelmed by them. I started the coffee pot. I made the bed. As soon as I heard Isaac talking in his crib, I changed him and fed him his bottle. I jotted down grocery and shopping lists. I dressed Aaron and cooked him a breakfast of French Toast with strawberries. When Amparo walked into our Upper Westside apartment at 8 a.m., I took Aaron to Bank Street on the No. 1 uptown. Once Aaron was settled in his classroom, I took the No. 1 downtown to 72nd Street and boarded the M-72 cross-town bus to the hospital on York Avenue and 67th Street. It was a morning of trains and buses and marching quickly through the crowds in Manhattan. I was sweaty, I was frazzled, but the long bus ride allowed me to recover. I couldn't wait to see Laura.

Laura was in a corner room on the newly renovated tenth floor reserved for breast cancer patients. The first day after surgery, her parents and I watched Laura breathe for eight hours. She drifted in and out of consciousness, and barely moved. Different teams of doctors visited the room, drew the drapes around her bed and checked Laura's progress. Laura's father and I asked a few questions. We were waiting for the final pathology report on the thirty lymph nodes Dr. Borgen had removed during surgery. Only after a careful analysis in the lab would we know, without a doubt, whether all of her nodes were cancer free. The surgeons said we would get the results in a few days.

Dr. Hidalgo's team inspected the blackish patch of skin with bad circulation. Dr. Hidalgo asked the nurses to apply a nitrate solution to heal this patch of skin. Another nurse told us Laura's job the next day would be to sit up and move into a chair for as long as Laura could stand it. The faster she moved her body, the quicker her recovery would be. But Laura was in agony. I peered at the drains to remove fluid from her abdominal and chest incisions. Her face was ghostly white, her breathing labored. Laura's eyes fluttered open, and she forced herself to smile wanly whenever she focused on the faces and flowers in her room. She did not say much that first day after surgery.

I thought about transferring Laura to a private room and placed a request to do it. But I changed my mind. Her room had a panoramic view of the Chrysler Building and mid-town Manhattan. The corner room was a junction of doctors checking Laura, nurses adjusting her IV and painkillers, janitors and laundry staff and friends and family of the patient sharing the room with Laura, a woman in her fifties who had undergone a mastectomy too. Laura's roommate was cheery and loved to dress up and chat with her husband, whose solicitous attention reminded me of my father. I thought we were lucky to share the room with her. A few doors down the hall, other patients wailed in agony, one was angry and loud and her family was the same way. Encouraged by all of us, Laura breathed into a plastic contraption with a blue cylinder to avoid the ill effects of anesthesia.

Laura's father repeatedly checked her pain relief medication. One of his doctor friends at Memorial, a pain relief expert for cancer patients, also paid a special visit to Laura's room. I thought having Laura's father at Memorial, who is a neurologist specializing in Alzheimer's disease, was a comfort for Laura. Despite the occasional disagreements I have had with him over the years, I know he is a good father. My mother-in-law stayed by Laura's bedside for nine days. When Laura took a few tentative steps, her mother, who has bad knees, guided Laura to the bathroom, a "walk" of eight feet that seemed an unconquerable expanse.

I could only imagine the pain Laura endured. Perhaps if I had been severely wounded in battle, I would have appreciated the depth of her agony. Two days after the surgery, I sat in a pink vinyl chair next to Laura and answered phone calls from friends, family and co-workers. Dr. Hidalgo's team arrived to check Laura's progress. Hidalgo asked Laura if we wanted to see the results of her breast reconstruction. I looked at Laura nervously, who nodded, and I stepped behind the curtains around the bed. At first, I almost gasped. A giant gash intersected her abdomen, where the ovaries had been removed and where the tissue had been taken for the TRAM flap. The wound was jagged and purple. As Laura would say years later, the doctors had "filleted her." Yet as I allowed my eyes to linger on Laura's wounds, I also noticed the incisions were neatly made. Her new breast was also purple and swollen, but it was perfectly shaped. I could not believe even skillful doctors could achieve such results by moving and shaping your muscles and skin like clay.

Laura was also relieved by what she saw, because she had chosen an uphill road. The recovery from the TRAM flap—with the incision and the abdominal muscle's new position and the movement of tissue to the chest area—would be lengthier and more arduous than, say, if Laura had opted for an implant or for no reconstruction at all. But now she could see her choice had been worth it. The patch of skin the doctors had worried about was better.

Laura's surgery had been on Monday, April 13th, and that Friday we heard the news about the lymph nodes from Dr. Borgen. The final pathology report revealed three lymph nodes positive, with microscopic bits of cancer. We were devastated. An ominous shadow blotted out the emergent sun. Positive lymph nodes meant the cancer could have escaped beyond her breast to Laura's vital organs. We had expected the lymph nodes to be free of cancer, because that had been the preliminary indication. Dr. Borgen, I noticed, felt bad he had given us that hope on the day of surgery. But it had not been his fault. The nodes had not been enlarged, and the surrounding tissue had appeared normal when he removed the thirty nodes.

Yet in this battle against breast cancer, what often seems fine and appears hopeful can prompt you to soar beyond what is really there. You have to wait for the tests, for the careful analysis, before you can trust your escape from this enemy. Even then test results may encourage hope, but something else, a new discovery, may question and reverse the validity of those first results. It is nearly impossible to check your emotions, because you yearn for a good result and perhaps selectively rationalize facts to gain that in your mind. I do not think a patient and her family should be pessimistic, in order not to be surprised by bad news. That attitude would be bad for the psyche, the immune system and morale. Perhaps it is better to be cautiously optimistic, still ready to fight the battle wherever it takes you.

These dramatic ups and downs were difficult to bear, and after Borgen's news Laura and I took a step back and steeled ourselves for a long campaign against her cancer. We had not expected any lymph nodes to be positive, but this was our reality. We had no choice but to face it.

Dr. Borgen reassured us that not only had the positive nodes not been enlarged, but those nodes had also been adjacent to a cancerous lump removed during the mastectomy. The nodes farther away were free of cancer. Maybe the cancer had begun to spread, but had not traveled far, and we had found it just in time. Also, the cancer had been next to Laura's skin. Borgen recommended radiation treatment to kill cancerous cells that might have reached the skin. The doctor mentioned a study with patients having similarly placed breast cancer. In over one hundred cases, not one patient had experienced the metastasis of breast cancer to the skin. Radiation treatment would ensure this good result. The breast surgeon also recommended only light chemotherapy because of the mitigating factors: the small number of positive nodes, the microscopic bits of cancer in these nodes and their location in relation to the cancerous lumps in the breast. Dr. Maria Theodoulou, Laura's oncologist, however, would be adamant about Laura having a full and even aggressive chemo regimen.

Each doctor approached cancer from his or her specialty. It should not have been a surprise that the breast surgeon might have one idea about chemotherapy and the oncologist another. They studied the disease from different perspectives, and each cancer was as specific as each patient. To expect "one right answer" was to expect too much. The amount and kind of chemotherapy for Laura, or any patient, was a matter of professional practical judgment. But "one right answer" has a seductive appeal when you are in a nightmare and desperate to return to a life without dread. In our battle against breast cancer, mathematical probabilities, not mathematical certainties, were as close as we could get to knowing if Laura would survive for years. Aggressive chemotherapy, according to Theodoulou, would increase Laura's chances of long-term survival.

That weekend I stayed with the children while Laura remained in the hospital with her mother at her side. We talked on the phone, and Laura was already walking brisk laps around the tenth floor. But I could not see her for two days. The children also needed me; I had seen them only at dinnertime for a week. Amparo was also exhausted after a week of extra long days and needed the weekend to recuperate. But I also wanted to give Laura *ánimo* for her recovery. I felt utterly torn in two. The time and distance from Laura was a chasm over which I remained rent.

When I did return to Memorial on Monday morning, Laura had become desperate to leave the hospital. Her pain was manageable, but Hidalgo wanted Laura to heal properly before discharging her. I brought two movies for Laura and escaped with her to a roof deck I discovered at the hospital. Laura sunned herself and was relieved; I also sneaked in Chinese food. After seven days, she hated the hospital food, the fragrance of the flowers (so I threw them out) and the sickly pleasantness of the pastel colors in her room. Laura was an animal trapped in a cage. I urged the doctors to tell us when she could be discharged.

Meanwhile, we rode the elevators to the sunlit lobby of the waiting room, IV pole and all. It was like playing hooky from school. Laura sat on a black couch, where I had once waited to hear the news from her surgeon. But instead of staring at the information desk and the update nurse as I had done, Laura faced the opposite way, toward the picture window. She drank in the panorama of trees covered with minty green leaves and the bright yellow taxis racing across the avenue. She wanted her life back. Laura munched on chocolate cookies and Godiva chocolates I brought from the Upper Westside. We lingered in the lobby for a while. Each minute revived Laura's spirit. The sunlight and the city's heartbeat seeped into her pores and replenished her. When we returned to her room, Laura was informed this night would be her last at Memorial. I remembered Laura whooped with joy. More than anything else, she wanted to be with her little boys.

# Letter to my Young Sons: Part Three

OUR APARTMENT WAS SUNNY AND QUIET WHEN LAURA AND I returned from Memorial Sloan-Kettering. During the taxi ride home, I could see that every bump on the pothole-covered streets of Manhattan caused Laura to wince with pain. She held her breath much of the way home. Walking to our building's front door, she was doubled over and unable to look at our doorman in the face. Once inside our apartment, Laura collapsed on our bed, faint, her face gray and pale, and shut her eyes. Amparo was picking up Aaron at Bank Street with baby Isaac.

At 3:30, I heard the door's deadbolt snap open. Aaron sprinted into the room, his eyes on fire and almost jumped on our bed before I stopped him with a hug. He grinned from ear-to-ear, eagerly glancing at Laura on the bed. I reminded him to be gentle with his mother. Laura hugged him, protecting her right breast with her arm, and kissed him. Big tears welled up in Aaron's brown eyes. "Mama's home!" he yelled excitedly and told Laura about his day at school. Amparo escorted one-year-old Isaac by the hand and released him at the foot of our bed. Isaac climbed onto it, like a small bear, and snuggled next to his mother. He rubbed his downy head of hair against her shoulders, his tiny hand gripping her arm. Laura turned her head and kissed Isaac, who did not move for a long time, lost in a trance next to Laura. I stayed close to all of them, because I knew how fragile Laura was.

One hour at a time. One day at a time. Laura gradually recuperated from her long day of surgery. Gone was the frantic look in her eyes, the terror of being trapped where she did not want to be. For the first few days, Laura alternated between lying on the bed and sitting on our navy blue couch. She was in acute pain and moved delicately. She read the newspaper, frequently napped with big pillows propping her legs and head or shuffled with tiny, granny-like footsteps around our apartment. She read stories to Aaron and Isaac.

Incredibly Laura began to take a few business calls in the morning. I helped her install Lotus Notes on our computer so she could check her e-mail and keep in touch with her colleagues at Chase. Dozens of electronic messages waiting for her were heartfelt get-well notes from friends, bosses and even rivals. The toughest, most competitive of the Wall Street crowd.

Laura returned home on April 22nd, nine days after her surgery. Her life inside our apartment on Manhattan's Upper Westside was enduring the discomfort from her operation and regaining her basic mobility. At first she shuffled only a few steps to the bathroom, to the kitchen and to sit on the sofa before she was exhausted. With every sudden move, Laura grimaced with pain. She moved unsteadily, her eyes riveted on the floor in front of her. The abdominal muscle that had been stretched to provide live tissue for Laura's new breast was sore and tugged at her if she straightened her back. I imagined it was like a giant rubber band that stretched from her abdomen to her reconstructed breast. The doctors said it would take time before the muscle loosened up and reconfigured itself to its new position. At night Laura slept face up, in a U-shaped position, her blue pillows behind her, and more pillows under her legs. The right side of her body was black and blue. A giant gash crossed her abdomen where the ovaries had been removed and tissue rearranged for her new breast. The first days and nights Laura endured tearful bouts of pain. But in the morning when Aaron and Isaac ambled into our bedroom, she smiled and said she was better.

My parents arrived from El Paso, Texas, the second week after Laura returned home. My mother cooked *flautas*, *entomatadas*, stir-fry chicken and Mexican rice, and my father, a retired construction engineer, created engineering projects with Aaron. Miniature cities of wooden blocks, trip-wire traps with string, and roads, tunnels and bridges. Isaac read picture books with Laura; *Mike Mulligan and his Steam Shovel* was his favorite.

In the morning, while Laura showered and I escorted Aaron to Bank Street, Amparo entertained Isaac and my father and mother ate breakfast at City Diner on Broadway. To rejuvenate themselves, my parents strolled to Riverside Park. My mother loved the boardwalk from 81st Street and to 72nd Street. She has always cherished the water, and the Hudson River is one of the most impressive rivers in the world. My father told me, months after returning to Texas, that my mother often cried for Laura at the river. My parents, who are surprisingly adventurous in cities like Madrid, Athens, and Tel Aviv, discovered the Catholic church on 82nd Street and Broadway, which has a Spanish mass on Sundays.

My parents who are really simple folk from the country —*gente del rancho*, they proudly declare—had always accepted Laura as their daughter. From the first day Laura spoke Spanish to them in Ysleta (and volunteered to unload bricks from my father's pickup), my parents have admired her. Now in New York, they saw Laura rarely complain about her pain. They saw how she cajoled Isaac onto the sofa with her, for she could not follow him. Every day she forced herself to walk a bit further, sit at the dinner table a bit longer, until fatigue over-whelmed her. My father and mother had always loved Laura. But in New York they elevated her to a heroine of mythical proportions. "Lá-u-rah," they would exclaim in Spanish, as if the very name commanded only silence afterward to appreci-ate the standard by which everyone else would be measured. But a person could be a "hero" in an ordinary sense, with her quiet struggle to survive and love: Laura just wanted desper-ately to live.

One day I accompanied Laura outside our apartment. We strolled around the block on 86th Street as she clutched her chest for protection. I was in front like an offensive tackle, watching that no hurried New Yorker bumped into her. Her abdomen was sore, her breast tender. We navigated our way around the block, allowing the foot traffic to go around us. The fourth week after returning from the hospital, Laura strolled with the children and Amparo to Riverside Park. Laura overextended herself and nearly fainted at the playground. Amparo was terrified, but they sat down for a while, on top of the hill overlooking the Hippo Playground, in the shadows of the oak and maple trees. Eventually they made it home.

Laura never felt sorry for herself. I accompanied Laura to her first doctor's appointment after the surgery. Hidalgo and his staff marveled at how swiftly Laura walked around. A while ago, Theodoulou had told me our greatest challenge would be to get Laura back into her life and to fight depression. Those surviving breast cancer possess an aggressive attitude about conquering this foe, or at least do not dwell on it too much. These reactions to a health crisis affect the patient's immune system, and can help or hurt her chances of survival. If the patient gives up, in some manner her body also gives up on her.

While Laura regained her strength, I helped her dress, I cared for the children after Amparo left and I encouraged Laura to sleep as much as possible. But as she became stronger, I pushed Laura to help feed Isaac. When Laura could dress herself, I did not offer to bring her clothes anymore. Soon Laura began to cook breakfast while I woke up the boys and dressed them. I was not a taskmaster, but I was pushy. I wanted Laura to regain her self-confidence; I wanted her to do as much as possible for herself; I wanted her to feel worthy. After a few weeks, it was time to get up, and time to get going.

Two weeks after Laura's surgery, we met Theodoulou to discuss Laura's chemotherapy. From the beginning, Dr. Theodoulou argued for aggressive chemotherapy for several reasons. Laura's tumor had been large and aggressive with significant necrosis, which meant that the tumor had quickly consumed the tissue around it. The cancer had also spread to her lymph nodes, however microscopically. Finally, Laura was young and able to withstand a full treatment of chemotherapy. If Laura had been seventy years old, Theodoulou might not have recommended this option. If we wanted to improve Laura's probability of surviving not just a few years, but many decades, then aggressive chemotherapy would grant us that statistical edge.

Theodoulou did not have to argue hard to convince us. We knew she had helped us attain the best doctors for Laura's surgery. The blond, cheery Theodoulou had always been frank, intense and intelligent. Laura asked many questions about chemotherapy. What drugs would she take? For how long? How debilitating would these chemical attacks be on her body? What effect would chemotherapy have on her immune system, white blood cells and memory?

To some questions, Theodoulou said she did not have the answers. One choice was whether to opt for a more aggressive four-month treatment, chemo drugs in two-week intervals or a six-month treatment of chemo, with a full compliment of drugs every three weeks. Another choice was the sequence of drugs: Adriamycin and Cytoxan (usually taken together), and Taxol ("A-C-T" chemotherapy). Dr. Theodoulou summarized the latest research on both the timing and sequence of drugs. Different studies had been inconclusive about the best options. Several studies, with different drug combinations of timing and sequence, were currently being conducted. Also, each choice had different implications for Laura. If she decided on the quicker treatment, she would be finished sooner. Laura did not want to suffer through six months of chemotherapy hell. Theodoulou also wanted Laura to undergo radiation treatment after chemotherapy. Laura wanted not only to aggressively attack her cancer, but also to have everything behind her.

But the intensive chemo treatment would be harsher on Laura's body. She would need to inject herself with Neupogen every night, to prompt her body to replace the white blood cells destroyed by the chemo. Only with this injection would she be able to endure the two-week cycles of toxicity. The less severe three-week treatment would allow the body to recover on its own, without Neupogen. Each patient also reacted differently not only to Neupogen, but to the A-C-T regimen. Some patients could not tolerate the quicker, more aggressive therapy, even with Neupogen. Others soldiered through the quick chemo week after week.

We were not experts; we did not know how to make the right choices. But we trusted Theodoulou. Laura and I were grateful Theodoulou had been clear about what were facts and what were weak or inconclusive opinions in the research. Laura asked Dr. Theodoulou what, in her best judgment, would be the best course of treatment. Without hesitation, Theodoulou said, "ACT in four months." Laura's life was in Theodoulou's hands. The doctor had brought us to consider the research and weigh the options. At the crucial moment, when Laura and I could not make a choice, Maria Theodoulou did not flinch. I was relieved the doctor was on our side.

On Wednesday, May 20th, ten days before returning to work, Laura began chemotherapy. I accompanied her to the first treatment, because we had no idea how Laura would feel after the infusion of Adriamycin and Cytoxan. Laura was nervous, and I wanted to be the one to bring her home. The night before Laura took Decadron, a powerful anti-nausea drug needed the first four days of each two-week treatment. Decadron often caused anxiety, so Laura also needed Activan to counteract the Decadron. At 2 p.m., for four days after each Wednesday treatment, Laura also took Zofran, another anti-nausea and anti-vomiting drug. On the Saturday after the Wednesday injection of Adriamycin and Cytoxan, and for the next eight days, Laura injected herself with Neupogen to prepare her body for the next round. If Neupogen did not succeed in producing enough white blood cells in Laura's body, chemo would have to be postponed for a week. Inside of Laura, I imagined a bubbly cauldron of drugs to kill the cancer, drugs to control her reaction to the drugs that killed the cancer and drugs to prep her body to take more drugs to kill the cancer. What in the world would happen to Laura amid these reactions and counter-reactions? To keep track of her drugs, Laura received a chemo calendar.

We felt intimidated and confused. But what choice did we have? Under the two-week chemo regimen, we did not have time to think. Maybe this was inadvertently beneficial. We were worried that a small, unobservable cancer lurked inside Laura's body. We listened to the doctors, took notes and readied ourselves for this scary ride. This was the only way out of permanent fear.

The special waiting room for patients in chemotherapy at Memorial has pastel colors, soft sofas and calm, helpful staff. One nurse called it the "Day Spa" of Memorial Sloan-Kettering. But in this spa, many women were bald. Others whispered in low, anguished tones. A few burst into tears for no reason, or shouted at nurses for the slightest delay. Frantic eyes were everywhere. This façade of soft colors and cool pleasantry, suffused with an explosive tension, became the norm for us.

Laura sat in a cushy recliner chair that was inside an open-door booth with medicines, poles for IVs, magazines and a sink. A nurse found one of Laura's thin veins below her elbow, taped an intravenous tube to her arm and dripped in an array of anti-nausea medicines, including more Decadron. Once Laura was prepped for chemo, it was time for Adriamycin. But this red drug was so caustic on the skin and veins that it could not be dripped in slowly. Two big red syringes with Adriamycin were pushed through the intravenous tube by the nurse in two minutes. Laura closed her eyes. Her arm trembled.

The nurse then attached the Cytoxan drip to an IV pole above Laura's head and gently thumped the intravenous tube to open another connection into Laura's veins. Colorless Cytoxan dripped into Laura's arm for an hour. The Wednesday rounds of Adriamycin and Cytoxan lasted ninety minutes. Laura was nauseous by that evening. When she later took Taxol, that drug dripped into Laura's arm for four hours, and caused her yearning-for-the-bed fatigue. Often on a Thursday night after her rounds of A-C chemotherapy, Laura vomited repeatedly at home. Theodoulou adjusted and readjusted the anti-nausea drugs to help Laura.

Laura's hair fell out in clumps after her second round of Adriamycin and Cytoxan. She shaved it off at the urging of her chemotherapy support group. Arranged by Memorial, the group formed a vital community to counteract Laura's loneliness and fear. Many in this group had already undergone the same treatments as Laura's, some with more, and others with less, positive lymph nodes. A few like Laura were at the beginning of chemotherapy. The women supported each other, chatted about work and exchanged tips on where to find the best wigs. They discussed their families and relationships, and often cried together. For Laura, these women became like a second family. Every Thursday they met for lunch, and Thursday evening Laura returned home and recounted their conversations and greatest fears. Laura's best friend in the group would die of breast cancer two years later.

Laura's chemotherapy continued from the end of May until September. This meant that Laura's wig came off on weekends. It was simply too hot to wear during the summer. She donned a scarf or a turban. At work, a few Chase colleagues complimented her on the new "hairstyle." Her close friends knew about Laura's struggle against breast cancer, but others were convinced Laura had changed her hair. The wig was that good. She had chosen the wig from a shop on the Upper Westside catering to actors, a tip from her support group. Our health insurance even picked up the tab. Laura's wig was that extra element that boosted her spirit and encouraged her to believe she was regaining her life.

During our summer of chemo, we could not travel anywhere, because Laura, with her lowered white blood cell count, was susceptible to getting sick. We revved up the air conditioners in our apartment, visited the air-conditioned Met, the Cloisters and the Bronx Zoo with Aaron and Isaac. We drove to the New York Botanical Garden to bask in the sunshine and flowers, a trip that rejuvenated Laura like no other. Through the forest of trees and magnificent lawns, amid the shadows and sunbursts, we discovered the secret alcoves of nature. I saw the world through Laura's eyes: green, ubiquitous green, the green of life. I wondered whether these "shots of green" were not as effective as the Neupogen in increasing Laura's white blood cell count.

At work, Laura purposely downplayed her fight against breast cancer. She did not want to be left "out of the loop." She wanted to return to her career as a banker. Many of her colleagues and all her managers already knew about Laura's chemotherapy. They knew that every other Wednesday Laura underwent another round of treatments and she would be at the doctor most of that day. Occasionally a few mentioned that Laura seemed exhausted. A couple of Latin American clients called Laura regularly to inquire about her health. In a quiet way, Laura appeased their unspoken worries about her health and career, and her colleagues at Chase gave Laura the room to take care of herself. They met in the middle. Laura, with a brave face, missed remarkably only one day (besides her chemo Wednesdays) during her four months of A-C-T chemotherapy. Meanwhile, her colleagues picked up the slack for her, with extra international travel. Laura had worked at Chase for ten years, and perhaps this was why she felt supported, instead of ignored or shunned, by her bank.

On a corporate recruiting trip to Yale's School of Management, Laura's alma mater, she glanced at the bathroom mirror and realized to her horror she had forgotten to paint her eyebrows in that morning. Laura hastily brushed them in with an eyebrow pencil and stepped out to continue interviewing potential MBA recruits with her colleagues. Had anyone noticed her hairless eyes? Laura never heard a word about it.

By late September, Laura was finished with her chemotherapy treatments and prepared for her last anti-cancer therapy: radiation. After the exhaustion and nausea of chemo, radiation was easy. Laura had a new right breast, after Hidalgo's reconstruction with the TRAM flap, so what was the point of radiating that breast? Even after a modified radical mastectomy, old tissue remains. The doctors can never remove every microscopic bit. In Laura's case, her cancer had been near the skin, and the possibility existed that her skin could harbor cancerous cells. Radiation treatment was the only way to prevent a local recurrence.

Two weeks after her final Taxol treatment, Laura entered Memorial Sloan-Kettering to be prepped for six weeks of radiation. The technicians created a mold of Laura's upper torso, which required her to be absolutely still for an hour, her right arm arched over her head like a ballerina. Laura's body position needed to be exactly the same every day for six weeks, so that the radiation machine, which rotated slowly around Laura like a refrigerator with blinking lights, targeted its beams on the same spots on her breast. Four small dots were tattooed on Laura's right breast. The machine was programmed to find these dots with infrared beams.

After this two-day preparation, Laura's radiation treatments began immediately. Monday through Friday. Fifteen minutes each day. From late September until October 30th. These treatments became a painless routine. Laura even said she enjoyed having the daily appointment at Memorial Sloan-Kettering, which gave her an excuse to leave work to take an autumn walk through Manhattan at mid-day. Once she arrived at Memorial, Laura changed in a prep room while the radiation team prepared the mold for her to lie in. As soon as the technicians were ready, Laura slipped into the open mold of her upper body, her arm over her head, and the technicians adjusted the machine to find the tattoo dots. The radiation treatments, two from different angles, lasted less than a minute each. Laura never experienced any discomfort during the radiation, and her curly brown hair grew back. After a few weeks, however, Laura's skin burned, as if she had spent too much time on the beach. The doctors told Laura to apply Aquaphor to help the skin heal. A week before Halloween,

Laura's skin blistered, and gauze kept her clothes from hurting her. She never missed one of her appointments at Memorial.

October 30th was the last day of Laura's radiation treatment. She had started her ordeal on April 13th, the day of her surgery, and had endured six months of nightmarish anxiety and severe pain through a gauntlet of therapies we hoped would stop her breast cancer forever. Laura cried so much the last day. She was elated it was over. She realized nothing more was left to do against her cancer. Her next checkup would be in a few weeks. For the first time in six months, we had no battle plan to follow. No anti-cancer therapy. No next round next week to dread and endure. Suddenly there was nothing more to do. The time in front of us was ours again. It was hard to believe. We had been climbing and battling to the top of one hill after another, and the terrain had changed and become flat and eerily quiet. Our legs and lungs waited, wanted to climb, but only a green meadow lay before us.

At the beginning of our ordeal, we had abandoned ourselves to whatever was necessary to fight Laura's cancer. Laura's agonizing recovery from surgery, her gritty survival through chemotherapy and the denouement of radiation had propelled us through the darkness we had entered. We had steeled ourselves for one essential task after another. We had been fighting for so long. But now it was time to survive outside. It was time to take a step back. It was time to take a step forward. The only weapon left against Laura's cancer was our hope for the future.

Laura needed two months to regain her full strength after radiation. Her body was exhausted. Her hair grew back quickly. Once in December, when Laura walked into Theodoulou's office, the doctor glanced at Laura's wig and told her to stop being "a chickenshit" and take it off. Laura was finished. Laura had done everything asked of her. She could stop concealing her battle against breast cancer. Laura was a survivor.

At work that week, Laura finally removed her wig and slipped into the Chase corporate headquarters with what looked like a buzz cut. Her secretary, who knew about Laura's chemo and radiation but had somehow not understood Laura had been wearing a wig for months, exclaimed, "You cut off all your hair!" A colleague walked into Laura's office and shared a story about a friend undergoing chemo. Throughout the day, Laura received supportive e-mails from other Chase friends. After a few days, she stopped sprinting to the bathroom to avoid bumping into colleagues in the hallways. Laura got used to her hair, and so did everybody else. On the street, she could delight in the cold breeze dancing across her scalp. I took a picture of Laura in December with her buzz cut, as she hugged Isaac on Florida's Sanibel Island, a brilliant orange sunset peeking above the Gulf of Mexico. Black storm clouds lingered on the horizon. Laura and Isaac have the most delicious of smiles on their faces.

Laura met frequently with Theodoulou and her other doctors, including Borgen and Hidalgo, for a series of blood tests, to check on the healing of her right breast, for physical exams of both breasts, for her annual mammogram, to renew her prescription of Tamoxifen. The quarterly blood tests were important, and stressful, because they measured enzymes that indicated the presence (but not the location) of cancer in Laura's body. Laura and I prayed these "marker tests" would be normal, and they were for month after month. When Laura felt a persistent ache in her hip, Theodoulou immediately ordered a complete bone scan. One of the most common places breast cancer can spread is a patient's bones. Any metastasis is devastating news, and immediately worsens her long-term odds of survival. But Laura's results were negative. Maybe, Theodoulou said, it was arthritis again.

The conventional thinking had once been that if a breast cancer patient did not have a recurrence in five years, then she was "cured." Now I had heard and read that the ten-year mark was crucial. But really, these were not magic numbers in any way, but statistical milestones used by cancer experts who study breast cancer survivors and what would probably happen to them after so many years without a recurrence. Every year without the cancer's return was a victory. The more years a patient was free and clear, the greater her chances would be her bones would ache but only because she was nice and old.

Postscript: Aaron and Isaac, I wrote this letter to you so that one day you would understand how brave your mother had been during that dark, difficult year in 1998 and how we survived together. Most importantly, we are still here. Laura, your mother, is still here. It has been three years since she was diagnosed with breast cancer and had surgery to remove it. She has had no recurrence. Laura still sees Dr. Theodoulou every three months, for more checkups and blood tests. But your mother is okay.

Encouraged by the good results we have received up to this point, we have slowly regained our precious quotidian fantasy. We traversed the black void that engulfed us at the beginning of our fight against breast cancer. We started believing again, believing the next day would be as good or better than today, believing we would have many days together, days to teach you everything you need to know, days for the adults to learn from their children, days to say "I'm sorry," and days to say "I love you."

But this battle has changed us forever. In the back of our minds, we harbor secret fears and more caution than optimism. We keep struggling and even succeeding against the odds. We have more days and we do not waste them. We do possess an eternal wound in a way, a wound that reminds us of the rarity and fragility of life. Our quotidian fantasy is now a new quotidian reality: vividly colorful days, days of curiosity, days bereft of many useless fears and petty ambitions, these days of wonder. In the glorious present, we above all love our two little boys. We have been excited to see you, Aaron, become a magnificent reader and storyteller, and you, Isaac, an incisive four-year-old rock scientist. Your mother and I are grateful each day we have with both of you.

# A Day Without Ideas

I IMAGINE THAT ONE MORNING I WILL WAKE UP AND HAVE NO ideas. One morning I will wake up and only see my wife slowly getting out of bed, just a few seconds before me. I will only see a tired woman rushing to make my son's lunch. Maybe I will also see her take a shower before she answers the calls of my other son, the baby. The little one sometimes sings in his crib, and one morning, maybe, I will only hear the sounds that woke me up. I will not hear him. I will not laugh at his attempt at melody. I will not see the brave woman who gets up to take care of him. I will not see anything at all but a tired world, a materialistic world, a quiet world, a non-world. My eyes will function, but I will not see much.

On this morning without ideas, I will take the four-year-old to school. Maybe I won't even talk to him, although he loves to tell stories as much as I do. In fact, I know he is a much better storyteller than I am. But on this particular morning, I will not hear his stories about Captain Morgan, the fearsome pirate. Once on the uptown subway to school, you see, we saw a poster for Captain Morgan's Spiced Rum. Every day we began telling Captain Morgan stories. One adventure would lead to another. After finding the treasure of the Lost Island, the poor captain would be blown off course by a storm. Then, every once in a while, Belzebub the evil octopus would run off with Morgan's treasure. I never mentioned the spiced rum to my son. But on this morning without ideas it will be as if I swigged the spiced rum, instead of just admiring the picture of the pirate. I will be catatonic almost, and I will not listen to my child and his great stories. Lumpaa, the friendly chocolate-munching monster? I will not know about him either.

On this day without ideas, I will probably not even call my wife just to hear her voice, even though I know she is busy at work. What would be the point of it? I know she took her Tamoxifen. I know she feels okay. Her hair has grown back, and is downy soft after the chemotherapy. Often when I call, there is really nothing important to say. We talk for a while. We talk about nice things. We tell each other we miss the other one. But it's rarely more than that. On this day I imagine, this day without ideas, I may not call at all unless I have something really important to say. I may even consider this call a waste of time.

So on this day, when it finally ends, after the children have taken their baths and they are falling asleep in their colorful room full of dinosaurs and lions and trains and puzzles and books, dozens and dozens of books, too many books, I will not sneak back in to hear them breathing. On this day, they are simply breathing. That is one of the things children do best. They breathe. Especially at night while they sleep. So on this day, as it turns into a dark night, my children will breathe, and I will not be sitting in the darkness hearing this wonderful sound like some nocturnal Buddha. It will simply be breathing, and I will not find it boring or exciting at all. It will simply be there, and I will not care. I will simply be there. On this day without ideas.

# Latinos Find an America on the Border of Acceptance

IN 2001, I HAVE SEEN A DEEPENING APPRECIATION OF LATINO culture throughout America—from literature to movies to popular music and art—and I have never been prouder to say I am the son of Mexican immigrants. When I went to college and graduate school in the Northeast years ago, I felt like an alien, in more ways than one. Imagine starting out without running water and electricity on the Mexican-American border and finding yourself, at eighteen years of age, in Harvard Square. Many things seemed strange to me on the East Coast, but the strangest was the almost complete Euro-centric view in everything from economics to politics to philosophy. I was determined to bust open closed minds, to point them toward Latin America, Latinos, especially Chicanos. The future of America, as I saw it.

Now that this future is arriving at a frenzied pace, now that the doors are starting to crack open for the popular acceptance of Latino culture, at least among the media elite, I see it's a pick-and-choose acceptance. There is little patience for discussing immigration issues and particularly the plight of day laborers and farm workers and other recent immigrants, who often can't yet defend themselves in English.

Why this dichotomy? Men and boys salivate over Salma Hayek as an absolute babe. Having "Lopez" or "Martinez" for a surname does not disqualify you anymore from being a top box-office draw or the best pitcher in America's pastime. The definition of an intense and intelligent American actor has to now include one Benicio del Toro. And yet, in each case, if they are not outright Latin American, they are the sons or daughters of Latin Americans, recent immigrants to the United States who have made it, and big. Shall we not also turn our eyes to those poor immigrants in this country who are still struggling against racism and poverty and language barriers, who might one day raise a son or a daughter even Hollywood or MTV can be proud of?

We still ignore the many issues of immigration while we have begun to embrace Latino culture because, first, this acceptance is at its beginning and most superficial phase. We can lionize the extremely beautiful and exceptionally talented Latinos, whether they be Chicanos from California or Puerto Ricans from the Bronx, more easily than we can have a meaningful discussion about the irrational fears of non-Latinos to the growing Latino community. These fears even come from the African-American community, where some believe in a zero-sum political game that the growth of Latino influence and power will translate into less influence and power for that community. The recent mayoral election in L.A., the first of the new millennium is a case in point.

Of course, in this superficial phase of acceptance, the television and film industries, eager to jump on a trend, often set the tone of debate. The media message is that Latinos are talented, they will be successful, they will make money and they are and will be good Americans. Just like us. And I have no doubt these things are happening now. Witness the explosion of the Latino middle class in the latest census figures. We lost the mayor's race in Los Angeles, but we won in San Antonio and El Paso. And Chicanos in LA will fight even harder for that political brass ring next time. But the time will come when we need to move beyond superficial acceptance in America. The time will come not just when we focus on how America is assimilating the variety and plurality of the Latino community, but when we understand that the United States, in the long run, will only be increasingly Latino. The issue of helping poor Latin American immigrants in the United States is not a "minority issue." It's an American issue, in the best sense of that term. When we move beyond a superficial acceptance meant to calm irrational fears, when we discuss immigration head on, then we will move toward a more profound sense of acceptance.

The constant flow of immigrants allows us to pick-and-choose success stories, especially from the first or second generation in the United States, another reason for this dichotomy between recent public and media acceptance of Latino culture and a lack of discussion and focus on the plight of poor immigrants. We can ignore, or even stigmatize, those who are now picking our apples or corn or grapes in the Hudson Valley, the San Joaquin Valley or the Ohio Valley. Unlike the episodic waves of Irish, Italian, and Jewish immigrants, the flow of Latin American immigrants to the United States will be a constant and significant stream into this country. Forever. We share a 2000-mile border with Mexico, and 500 million Latin Americans live south of that border. You can run away from these realities, or you can rage against them drunk with hate, or you can try to make it work, for all of us. What do you think is the best choice?

This constant flow of Latin American immigrants into United States also creates divisions within the Latino community, the third reason for this dichotomy between acceptance and rejection of American Latinos. I have seen with my own eyes how established immigrants—or their first- or second-generation children who sometimes don't know a word of Spanish anymore—are the first to call for the militarization of the border, or the first to turn their backs on the non-English-speaking construction worker who was mauled by thugs. Latinos, we can't reduce ourselves to such selfishness. The poor immigrant is part of *nuestra familia*. It's as simple as that.

Instead of succumbing to self-hate or self-racism, which unfortunately has been taught to all-too-many groups in the United States, we, Latinos, should show our country a different way. We should be proud of our heritage. And instead of being silent about the issue of immigration, we should be the first to help new immigrants join this American experiment.

The final reason for this dichotomous reality of American Latinos and Latin American immigrants is more complex, but no less significant. It relates to what will always be appealing and what will always be ignored by the media culture of America. As I see it, the media are at the apex of what is worst about materialism in American culture. Caricatures instead of characters. Fifteen-second sound bites instead of thoughtful debates. Pretty or scandalous images instead of thinking. In the literary field, my field of work, almost nothing is written about how Latin American immigrants survive and toil and often die in the United States. These images simply don't sell.

For this reason, I have often called for Latinos, particularly Chicanos, to define themselves, and not to let others, even the well-intentioned media, define who we are. That's why I have written stories about growing up on the Mexican-American border of El Paso, Texas. Stories about people who work and try to make a life and sometimes fail and sometimes succeed.

The quotidian reality of hard work and small successes and failures is the reality we mostly live in, but too often it is the reality ignored by the American media. So I don't mind that the wealthy and beautiful and talented Latinos are being accepted into the American family. But I do not forget where I came from. I do not forget who I am. I remember that there are others who are not photogenic or rich, those who may not know any English or may just be embarrassed by their accent. They are working hard and fighting just to stay alive. They've got more guts than most Americans I know on Manhattan's Upper Westside. They weren't born into the American Dream. They've traveled hundreds, even thousands, of miles just to be a part of it. They will never make the cover of *People Magazine*. But these immigrants are knocking on my door. And not only am I letting them in, but I am introducing them to my American friends so that they appreciate the full extent of *mi familia*.

Not long ago, I attended a children's concert by Pete Seeger at the Hudson Valley Writers' Center, where I am a member of the board of directors. I was there with my wife and two kids, and in the audience were also twenty children of migrant farm workers who had been invited to the concert as part of our outreach program. Pete Seeger is a folk legend, for good reason. Although he is no Jennifer Lopez, he jumped up and down and strummed his banjo, giving a spirited concert and connecting with the kids in Spanish and English. It was a small Sunday event, not flashy enough for any media to cover it. But crowded inside the small train station that is our writers' center, overlooking the Hudson River, we easily belonged together.

# The Father Is in the Details

MONDAY NIGHT . . . THE COUNTER CLEAN, WHILE THE DISHES drip-dry inside the dishwasher-qua-dish rack. I check the stove, fill the coffee pot with water, Bustelo coffee for eight cups in the morning, set the timer to 6:15. Before I sneak into bed in the dark, I also check the deadbolts, the chain, the turtle's heat lamp (the electrical cord should not be touching it) and the children's room, for air circulation, to hear if anybody's wheezing, to listen to Aaron and Isaac breathe. I pray I sleep through the night.

Tuesday. I receive a call from the nurse at the Bank Street School for Children: Aaron feels itchy. They call me since I am a writer, always available. Laura is a banker and earns the steady money. A kid in Aaron's class touched him, after eating brownies with walnuts. Touched and taunted him. That kid thinks it's a big joke Aaron has serious nut allergies. I talk to the nurse and Aaron. Aaron whispers he's nervous. Ten days ago Aaron ate a cookie at the dinner table. In a matter of seconds, his face reddened like a strawberry, and he wheezed and coughed to breathe. Off the charts, the doctor told us. Tiny drops of hazelnut, cashew, walnut oil prompted blisters the size of quarters on Aaron's forearm. When he ingests tree nuts, that is what happens inside his lungs, the doctor said. Aaron has only minor allergies to grass, trees and poppy seeds. Over the phone, I reassure Aaron the kid touching him will not trigger an allergic reaction. Aaron, I tell him, you have to eat the nuts for anything bad to happen.

After school, Aaron excitedly recounts his "moot court." He argued the "con" side of Peter Minuit, one of the Dutch directors of New Amsterdam, New York before it was New York. Aaron argued against the Dutch-owning slaves, and against their policies of granting too much land to rich "patroons." My older son will appreciate New Amsterdam and New York. But what will he know about El Paso, my hometown and Mexico, the land of my father and mother? We will soon be in Boston for Passover with Laura's folks, then with my family for Easter in Ysleta, my neighborhood on the Mexican-American border in Texas. Combo religions. Combo cultures. Don't get too confused, Aaron and Isaac. But they do not seem to be.

Aaron tells me about Peter Minuit and the "freedom-loving" Dutch. Freedom for them, but not for the Africans. The "right" to land in the Northeast, because the Dutch and the English granted themselves the "right of discovery" and the "right of proper titles." Read: I see, therefore I take, from the Lenape, Algonquin and other Native Americans who cannot read or write Dutch or English—I make reading and writing cudgels of conquest. I hope Aaron gives 'em hell at Bank Street. Unlike Aaron and Isaac, I feel trapped between Spanish and English, an heir of neither, in exile in both. I wonder if any of the Native American survivors felt like mistakes of history.

Isaac, my younger son, is tall. The tallest seven-year-old at Bank Street. After school, he has Science. Isaac is shy, unlike his ten-year-old brother, and asks to go to the restroom when he is jumping in place. Why does he wait? I have told him to ask the teacher if he can get a "drink of water" if he is too shy to ask her permission to go to the restroom. I have mentioned it to the Science teacher, and she will let him go, but sometimes Isaac waits too long. Isaac immerses himself in work uncannily. He has special abilities in mental math and can add three-digit numbers in his head. I cannot do that. I am proud of him and Aaron, my EB's, I call them. Excellent boys.

At home, Aaron practices the piano, and Isaac and I play H-O-R-S-E with the mini-basketball net and ball on his closet door. I beat him. Isaac is angry; I can see it in his eyes. He usually wins. Everybody has to learn to play fair. Win or lose, you should try your best and be a good sport. I say only that the game is over. He urges me to play volleyball across the beds with the mini-basketball. Perhaps he is growing up, maturing. Do I want him to grow up so quickly? We play volleyball, hitting the ball across the room on opposite beds. Isaac spikes the ball hard at me. I can't reach it, and he smiles hard at me. He is still angry. Still a kid, but older. Don't get too old too soon, my son. It is not worth it. Get angry when you lose. The problem is accepting loss too easily. I know plenty of writers like that. By bedtime, Isaac plants a goodnight kiss on my cheek. I love my little boys.

Wednesday. I am exhausted and faint. I awoke at 4:45 a.m. Don't know why. Too hot. Too much in my head. Today my eyes are rimmed by dark circles. I yelled at the kids to get their beds done, to get dressed and ready for school, when they were reading under the covers. I unleash these outbursts, I know, when I suffer another night of insomnia, when I have given up for the day, when I believe I am not a good writer. When I have given up on myself. Why do I find it easy to criticize myself and others, and create from criticism? Is it because I am a world-weary adult? Or because I was born dirt poor in Ysleta and survived at Harvard beset by self doubts? The voice, my voice, a wicked thunderclap, astonishing in its volume.

At breakfast, I take a step back and ask Isaac to help Aaron. Aaron will have a multiplication test soon. He thinks he's ready. I could "test" him, too, but my head is abuzz like a rotten log full of hornets. Besides, the brothers should find ways to work together. Isaac loves to be in charge and studies Aaron's sheet and finds how the two rows of factors meet for the answer. Occasionally Isaac does not allow Aaron enough time, or Aaron snaps at Isaac to hurry with another problem. But they work it through and that is what I want. I want them to be there for each other when Laura and I are not anymore. I know, I am planning my own replacement. One day they will be rid of this grumpy, overly strict father.

At school, I stay with Isaac in his classroom for a few minutes. He shows his homework to his teacher and finishes his measuring work for morning warm-up. He must choose and measure different objects. Isaac does a meticulous job, but is distracted by friends. Finishes measuring a ruler (!), an eraser, the base-ten-blocks bin, a book. Then orders the items from shortest to longest. He does his own work, and the teacher is pleased. When I am about to leave, he sits down to read Beverly Cleary and kisses me goodbye.

I walk up the stairs to Aaron's room on the third floor. I feel superfluous now. Aaron works independently. He reads his morning passage about different jobs in New Amsterdam, the assignment for morning warm-up. I read the passage too, in a distant corner. The rattle shaker is my favorite. Proto-policeman who roamed the village in New Amsterdam with a rattle, and shook it when he witnessed crime. Aaron also reads a poetry book. I remember how proud I was yesterday when he worked alone on his math homework and the challenge problem. Using the block method. Multiplying two three-digit numbers. Adding all the sums. The problems perfect. I checked the homework as he read in the living room. Did I know that much at ten?

I stop everything at 3 p.m. to pick up the boys after school. Aaron meets me in the fifth-floor library. Kisses and hugs in the stacks. His classmates are not around. Will I always receive so much affection from my children? Aaron carries his blue backpack heavy with homework, his violin, his red windbreaker. I ask him if he is hungry, or if he wants to get a drink in the basement cafeteria while we wait for Isaac. But Aaron would rather stay in the library. He checks out *The Golden Compass*, by Philip Pullman. Aaron has trouble finding young adult novels he has not yet read. I will pick him up in a few minutes.

I walk downstairs to pick up Isaac in after-school Chess. Through the window slit next to the door, I see Isaac take the queen and defeat his opponent, a boy in Aaron's class. I am proud of Isaac, one of the youngest in this program. He shakes hands with his partner and picks up his backpack and lime-green windbreaker. He tells me he beat another older boy, but lost his first match. The chess teacher says Isaac is progressing well and has found his place in the class. Aaron has a "great game" too, but gets silly with his friends in Chess III, loses focus and sacrifices pieces needlessly. I will mention to Aaron that silliness saps your power in chess.

On the fifth floor, Aaron gives Isaac a chess book he found in the library. The brothers hug each other. I am secretly thrilled. Excellent brothers and excellent boys. EBs squared. Aaron hands me a math test as we walk into our apartment. Twenty-nine right, out of thirty. I give him a big hug.

Thursday. In the morning, Laura, Aaron and Isaac rush toward me as I step out to pick up *The New York Times* and *The Wall Street Journal* in the hallway in front of our apartment door. They scream. A rat in the kitchen! My heart thumps hard inside my chest as I scan the floor. April Fool's Day! Oh man, they got me. Later, sweet revenge.

I take the kids to school again. Even on Manhattan's "sophisticated" Upper Westside, I am the rare father: I drop off and pick up my kids at school. I am resilient against the occasional pitiful stare I catch from a mother or nanny. I am like my mother: I make our household work well. I am proud of the work I do, I am more than exhausted because of it. I am also surprised at how many "modern" parents, men and women, do not respect this kind of work. I make sure the homework is done, provide a pleasant time to decompress after school and make healthy snacks. I've learned. It is indeed about sacrifice, and who's willing to do it, and who's good at it. To make a good home for my children, I have sacrificed the only thing that matters more than my family: I have novels in my head which I may or may never get a chance to write.

I have noticed many things from this perspective. Some parents pick up their children regularly, and maybe they shouldn't. Some parents don't want the "trouble," and send someone else. Rarely is that nanny terrific, often she is serviceable, and on occasion neglectful. It is simply what I see everyday. What matters is time with a child. What matters is adult adaptability to a child's point of view. Parenting is invisible like the air we breathe, but just as vital. Parenting is the hardest work you might do, and should be praised, but too often it is not. Am I a fool? Sometimes. But not for taking care of my kids.

As I walk home on Broadway after leaving the boys at Bank Street, I am thinking I cannot blow up today. That is my daily struggle as a father. When I yell at them, I show them the wrong way to handle pressure. It is always about an innocuous issue. I hate myself deeply when I yell, and their horrified little faces haunt me for days after I explode. My exhaustion is the fuse.

These words have helped me in a way. I put myself there, on the page, this impatient self, and attempt to step beyond it. What I want is to change my character forever. I want to be a good father. Nothing I think about and struggle to accomplish is more important.

Friday. Today Laura decides to take the kids to school. Thank goodness. I get a break. She handles the weekends, so I love having a free weekday morning. While Laura dresses, I hurry them to get their backpacks ready, to finish their breakfast, to comb their hair. Why am I so pushy? They get to school okay. Do not let your high expectations for them become burdens they hate to carry, I tell myself, turning on the computer to return e-mails. When I step back from the precipice before I lose control, these children will get the work done. If my expectations are negative or assume the worst at these moments, then the picture they will have of themselves will be as disobedient, lazy or disorganized children. My own father worked at a job he was reasonably good at but did not like, as a draftsman for a construction company. He sometimes came home bitter, at bosses who overworked him, at the sacrifices for his family and at sons who enjoyed a carefree life in English while he could not. At other times, my father walked into the kitchen, blueprints under his arm and helped me paint a puppet theater for school, or drew signs for my run for Sophomore Class President. As for me, I can't wait to pick up my boys after school today.

In the school lobby, Aaron tells me a few kids had to write letters today. Not him. A letter about how they did not respect someone else, or how they interrupted or disrupted the classroom, and what strategies they will use to prevent a recurrence. Their parents must sign the letter and return it to the teacher the next day. Aaron relishes telling me how someone got into trouble. I have to ask him what happened or what did he do that was *good* today. Am I teaching him to focus only on the negative?

Isaac tells me he will be building a police station with a friend, for "Crate City." In Isaac's class, they are studying how neighborhoods work by visiting shops and museums and police and fire stations near Bank Street. For the end of the year, the kids will build their own neighborhood out of wooden crates. Their first question and assignment before they chose what would be in Crate City were to understand the difference between what a neighborhood needs and what it wants.

In the evening, the piano teacher arrives, and Isaac is first. At seven-years-old, Isaac is beginning piano and loves it. The teacher, a gregarious Russian, is tough, but agrees to teach Aaron and Isaac on our electronic keyboard. Isaac plays her a "song" he composed, with a moody, rhythmic feel. She focuses on his recognition of notes and basic songs to develop good finger technique. I am in our bedroom. I want my kids to talk to their teachers by themselves and develop their confidence and voice with adults.

Aaron is next, a much more advanced piano player. He works on "serious music," as the piano teacher regularly reminds him. When I hear Aaron play Beethoven's *Sonatina*, my heart actually flutters in my chest. For me it is breathtaking.

Saturday. I am sleeping late. Feel like a king. The kids are watching TV. Laura cooks breakfast for them. I rarely eat breakfast, a habit Laura is trying to break. She is also preparing a late lunch for a family we have invited for a swim. Their older child is in Aaron's class, and the younger in Isaac's. Laurita makes chicken *flautas*, Mexican rice and guacamole and tosses a salad, her specialties, and as good as my mother's. I make our bed and shower. I have to take Aaron to Taekwondo before lunch.

Aaron scooters to Taekwondo on Amsterdam Avenue about six blocks away. At the Dojang, he ties his yellow belt meticulously, finds his battered attendance card, buys a Gatorade, bows to the American and Korean flags on the wall and sits on the mat as he waits for his class to start. The head instructor today, an angular, gruff, bald black belt, encourages and pushes the students to exercise. Aaron warms up, with half-hearted jumping jacks, stretches. Partners sit down, spread their legs. First they have to jump over their partner's legs, flat and splayed on the mat. I am surprised how agile Aaron has become. They switch to pushups, with one partner gripping the other's legs in the air. Aaron is tough. When did my chubby ten-year-old become a pint-sized linebacker? The children get into four lines; the other black belts follow the head instructor and demonstrate the high and low kicks they want them to practice. Rapid-fire thud-thud. Like spidery machines. Bright shouts of "Kia!" and "Hi!" reverberate against the white walls.

After lunch, back at home, the kids and their friends swim in the pool in our building, with Laura and the other mother. The other father is a no-show. I stay in the apartment and clean up after the meal. It is only fair; Laura did all the cooking. I wash the dishes, put away the food. Under our table, on my knees, I wipe the crumbs and bits of lettuce and gobs of guacamole off the wooden floor. Maybe I am too fastidious. But why do a half-hearted job? Don't see the point in that. Either you care about who you are, and where you live, or you are just waiting to die. My mother is like that. A manic cleaner, always in motion, with an excess of energy that begs to be channeled into tasks. As a child, seldom did I ever see her idle. My mother, a Mexican immigrant.

Sunday. Wormhole. Discovered the Space Cadet Pinball on my new computer. Four million points. Sweet program. Kids watch Sunday morning cartoons. Laura will take Aaron to Taekwondo. I loved playing pinball as a kid. In front of Ysleta High School, I wasted hundreds of dollars in quarters at the Alameda Arcade.

I run before Laura leaves for Taekwondo. A dry wheeze escapes from my lungs. I am a slow jogger. Trying to keep the weight off. I have always worried that I might have a heart attack and nobody would ID me on the sidewalk. My body is an achy mess. The invulnerability of my youth—in El Paso, in Cambridge, in New Haven—has drained away one year at a time. I carry a credit card with me. I do finish five miles in Riverside Park.

Back home, I revel in the shower's hot water, for once rejoicing in the aches of my body. Laura leaves with Aaron for Taekwondo. Isaac knocks on the bathroom door and says he wants to play baseball. Last night, we watched half an hour of the Red Sox completing a three-game sweep of the Yankees. Isaac wants to be like Alex Rodríguez. I dress, but my body is creaky after my run. I pick up our baseball mitts. I think how "some guys wash up after work," in Bruce Springsteen's song "Racing in the Street," and "go racing in the street." This inspires me. Suddenly, a reprieve: it is raining.

Isaac and I run to the old racquetball court in our building. We play a game where I pitch to Isaac, and he hits it and runs to whatever base he can reach safely. An imaginary Isaac stays on that base, and the real Isaac returns to bat. In the second inning, Isaac slides into first like A-Rod yesterday, almost knocking my tooth out with the top of his head. But Isaac is safe. The Isaacs win 13-4. My son's face is sweaty, red and hot; he recounts the most exciting plays of our game, as mini-lore, while we wait for the elevator.

Monday. I take the kids to school. Later, get tickets to the Yankees-Red Sox game next Saturday. The boys will be thrilled. In town from Boston, Laura's brother and sister-in-law will join us. I walk to Food Emporium for eggs, milk,

Lemon Pledge, beef stew cuts, onions, low-fat Greek yogurt (Laura's favorite), a cantaloupe, bananas, small water bottles, Cheerios. Go to Duane Reade for toilet paper, paper towels, shampoo, liquid Tide. I am exhausted carrying four heavy bags. My fingers are blue. It's not even 11 a.m. and it's already too hot in New York City.

At home, I write, return e-mails, but I feel light-headed in front of my computer. I hope it is not my high blood pressure. Laura is angry I have avoided my annual checkup, because I want to lose weight before I see Dr. B. Dr. B is a good doctor, but I do not want to hear I need to lose weight and cut the salt out of my diet to lower my blood pressure. I know I should do these things, but I falter. My right leg is numb. Maybe I should take a walk. I have to pick up the kids at 3 p.m. That is one deadline I cannot miss. My life.

After school, Aaron has a playdate; I see him with a friend in the Bank Street lobby. I give him a Claritin I have saved in foil paper since I forgot to give it to him this morning. The pollen count is high today. His friend's caregiver is taking them. As I wave goodbye, Aaron yells back to me that he will do his homework before he and his friend start playing. Did I give him a look to prompt that? I am giving looks without knowing I am giving looks. As they walk to the street, I hope the nanny is as alert at each crosswalk as I would be. I am trusting you with my child, I say inside my head like a prayer, my stomach churning.

I meet Isaac in his classroom. He has painted his crate, the police station, black and white, but talks about spies. Wanted to call it the FBI and CIA, instead of the police station. A "claw" will pick up suspects by the head and implant a "microchip" in their heads and fingerprint them, Isaac tells me. The NYPD would love Isaac's "community police tactics." But I do not want him to become a cop. Too dangerous. What will happen if my boys are drafted to fight in a war? My infrequent nightmare. Dear God, a deal. Take me, sacrifice my life, if you're up there, with power over our puny affairs. But do not let harm ever come to my boys.

I pick up Aaron from his playdate, Isaac in tow. It is raining again. Aaron's nose is itchy and runny; his friend has guinea pigs, a rabbit, a dog. Tonight I will turn on the air conditioning to relieve his allergies, although it is early in the season. At home, we sit down for an early dinner, tired. Spaghetti and meat balls, with a side of broccoli. They watch an hour of Nickelodeon TV, and Aaron's allergies abate. I return an e-mail from a university that wants to invite me for "Latino Heritage Month" and update my website. I practice Aaron's multiplication facts with him.

Isaac rips open an Erector Motion System set, and we began to assemble one of the cars he likes on the box. After an hour, I hunch over the table to screw in a tiny nut and a tiny bolt at a right angle to another tiny nut and tiny bolt. My back spasms, and I ask Isaac if we can take a break. Aaron reads a comic book; Laura walks in from work. I lie flat on the living room floor and close my eyes and listen, in my darkness, to the kids in the other room with their mother. I remember how much I love my wife and my children, how spent my body feels, how I would love to obliterate myself by becoming the floor. I hear the raindrops thump gently against the window.

In the evening, everyone is asleep except me. I finish *A Portrait of the Artist as a Young Man*. I put the book next to our sofa, turn off the lights, except for the one in the kitchen. I open the door to the kids' room, and the air conditioning is humming, and Aaron and Isaac are breathing.

I see how being a good father is in the details. Learning from details. Reacting the right way to details. Thinking about what your children are saying to you. Listening. Doing. Exhaling when the details overwhelm. I leave the door open. In the kitchen, I wipe . . .

# Terror and Humanity

(This commentary was written on 9-11-01,
and appeared the next day in *Newsday*.)

THIS ONE IS FOR THE THOUSANDS OF INDIVIDUALS WHO DIED
yesterday. Those innocents. It's hard to write this, to write
anything. The fathers and mothers. The children. Brothers
and sisters. They died for somebody's idea of a just cause. But
you were simply killing innocents, can't you understand that?
The children visiting the top of the World Trade Center were
simply looking at the view. The mothers who jumped out of
these skyscrapers, in desperation, did not know about your just
cause and did not care about politics. These innocents who
died are America, and those who will mourn them today will
rebuild our great city and our great country in their honor. We
don't have a choice but to rebuild and try again to live in this
sometimes nightmarish world. In these thousands who died
amid an ordinary Tuesday morning that metamorphosed into
terror, we have a representation of America. But that does not
mean they bear any individual or collective responsibility for
your hate.

You hated them simply because they were a disembodied "America" in your mind, an abstract idea, something easy to hate because you had already categorized them into something distant, something you can't or won't touch, something far away you will not have any discourse with. A thing. For you, killing the Twin Towers was killing America. Killing buildings was equivalent to killing people to killing a country. All these "things" were the same, in your hate-filled mind, but you were wrong. You have killed innocents. You have killed individuals. You categorized us into this thing that you hate, you idealized us into something wretched and you went about trying to kill this idea-thing with your horrible acts. But you were wrong, and this is why America, this unique and wonderful land of diversity, this expanse of individuals working together, cannot be defeated by your hateful acts. We will rebuild our country, and we will always remember those innocents who died yesterday.

What I believe this Tuesday should teach us, if we can still learn anything in our deepest grief and shock, is that our ideas, when we turn them into hateful things, when we categorize innocents into being disembodied entities, these ideas and the minds that latch onto these idea-things for the sake of a warped clarity, they are at the root of what is evil. To be human is to engage with, to care about. To be human is to love another. To be human is to communicate with someone, even if you are only shouting at them. The most human of all is discourse. With nature. With other human beings. Even with other ideas. But when you prefer an island of clarity in your mind, when you don't want to be contradicted, when you don't want to defend your actions, then you will turn human beings, innocents, into things. And then it is so easy to kill these "things" in your mind.

But even if America, that America of individuals working together, was deeply wounded on this black Tuesday, even if thousands of us died because someone turned us into a thing to hate in his mind, America will not be defeated. We will get up again. We will grieve. We may even hate for a while, too, because our anger has reached unimaginable levels. But we will fight against our hate, we will argue against it, in our own minds, and we will finally put it aside as something at the root of evil, where we do not want to go. And then we will win our fight to be human. One day in the distant future, one day perhaps far away, we will have a good day when we don't cry anymore about those thousands of innocents who died yesterday. We will never forget them, but we will go on with caring about, loving and arguing with each other. And then, on another clear and sunny day, when we should be taking our children to the park or to visit a famous skyscraper or simply getting them ready for their first week of school, we will be wounded again by someone who has not bothered to escape the idea-things in his mind. And never shall we give up on ourselves. Never. This one is for the thousands of individuals who died yesterday. I wish I had known every single one of them.

# Trapped

I NEED TO WORK. I DROP THE KIDS OFF AT THE BANK STREET School for Children and linger for a few minutes with Isaac, the younger child, and pretend I am still needed in his 9/10's classroom (i.e. for nine- and ten-year-olds). Aaron had left me in the lobby and only wanted a quick kiss and a look to reassure him that I am not angry at him for another offense. He is quick to notice, and perhaps I have been harder on him. But he is at once more aggressive and sensitive, and so I react quicker to him than with Isaac. This laptop, the Taekwondo clothes I carry like a mule outside of Bank Street, across Broadway, to Oren's Coffee, where I get the regular blend, extra light. Why doesn't Laura drop off the kids anymore? I am tired, and I have just begun my day. Maybe I am just pretending to be a writer too.

At Columbia, the African-American guard—bald, with thin, round glasses, and a snappish demeanor—glances at my ID card. Usually he studies it like a philosophical text, but not today. He waves me in. What did the trick? The striped oxford

97

shirt, or the new black windbreaker? Perhaps the ridiculously large laptop? But Mr. Smiley-Who-Is-Not-Ever-Friendly does ask me what's in the bag, and I tell him Taekwondo clothes (not mine, but Aaron's, for after school). He waves me into Butler Library. I need to work; I need to focus. Why haven't I written five books already? Why do I want to?

I find an enclosed desk on the first floor, in the reference area, a huge room, with thirty-foot ceilings, often jam-packed with undergraduates during exams, otherwise empty. I notice the young, beautiful and raw women. Women with tattoos. Women badly dressed, yet possessing young bodies. Women with thick library glasses and prim hair, yet with furtive glances. But surprisingly I do not linger on them today; I have to work. Maybe I am getting old. This room, cavernous, bleakly lit and quiet, is about being alone, or pretending to be alone, or wanting to be alone to jumpstart the mind into an elusive immortality. My desk is like a small temporary tomb, claustrophobically enclosed, deeply dark brown, for a body trying to block out the world. Small oak walls encircle my perspective and force me to focus on my work. Why do I do this to myself? Yet this self-deception usually works, with only one problem. I have access to the Internet.

At my tomb-desk, the Ethernet connection, electricity and wireless signals reach my laptop like outstretched, bony fingers. The computer is a window beyond these self-imposed walls. I am tempted. I return e-mails; I secretly hate anything from the Hudson Valley Writers' Center, because I am thinking of quitting their board. Sure, it's important to me. But other members are too tempted by commercial writing, by petty and destructive politics, and one who shall not be named is the most manipulative control freak I have ever met. She smiles in a passive-aggressive, Nixonian manner, and stabs me in the back yet again. I imagine driving a pickax through her skull. Another is rich, lazy and shameless, yet she can always charm the board with her Benjamins. Why do I waste my time with these people? I must be a masochist. I should be writing. I check my stocks, read news articles on My Yahoo! and glance at the headlines of the *El Paso Times*. I review, always with the ridiculous hope of the Lotto, whether my books are selling on Amazon.com. Rarely am I higher than 51,634th place. I pluck my eyebrows, notice an amorphous pain in my left lower abdomen (cancer? a hernia? intestinal blockage? an overgrown parasite?). My head throbs because I awoke at five in the morning with a sneeze, and I don't ever sleep well. I sit at my desk-tomb, but I am not writing. Why? I unplug the Internet and push my laptop away. The blue-and-white Word icon rests at the center of my desktop background, a rural dirt road into the forest. I am going nowhere and I have a picture of it.

I slump into another chair behind me in front of a Columbia computer, trying to escape my self-disgust. I punch my name into the Factiva database to see if I exist as a writer worth his salt, not a waste, not a victim of a casual drowning in this godforsaken sea. I am the Grand Poobah of procrastination. I return to my tomb-desk and avoid the eyes of a young student in a ponytail whose jeans are too tight and who has grinned at me from the foursome table a few feet away. I don't think she is flirting with me; she probably feels sorry for me. Refocused at my tomb-desk, I click on the jazzy, palpitating Word icon and sit down to work. My butt will not move, I tell myself, until I make progress. I hate myself, but then I force myself to work.

As I am rereading a chapter of my novel-in-progress, my right leg bounces up and down like a piston. I have always had this problem. Too much energy expended, consumed, needed. In high school, I remember a writing teacher, Bruce Lambert of the Blairstown Summer School for Journalism, lecturing me about how I had a problem with my leg, a certain lack of control, and too much nervousness, perhaps curable, perhaps not.

He donned a bow tie, New England to the core; I was a sixteen-year-old Chicano at a private school in New Jersey for a summer, confused. I didn't imagine smashing a pickax through his head, but instead smiled and stopped pumping my leg in class, embarrassed. But this leg problem, and my loins, won't leave me in peace. Yes, I think it's connected to my loins. I want to have sex all the time, or at least I think I want to have sex all the time. (Have old New England gentlemen lost their appetite for sex?) I have this warmth between my legs that causes my leg to jump, that prevents me from averting my eyes from luscious maidens, a warmth that seems a source of excess energy, anger and motion. Sometimes I want to run for five miles to cool it down. I could be staring at my Internet cable, and its connection to nothing, and my mind might turn to the warmth between my loins, to this energy wanting to explode. I imagine, look for, a tight blouse, or go back in time to a memory, or think about my wife. Yes, that's one benefit of my malady. I love being with my wife. I make her consistently happy (unless I have deluded myself). I am proud of that, not macho proud, just warm-in-the-gut proud to be able to please her. That's the productive use of this leg problem; that's what society expects of men. But there's still too much energy leftover at this tomb-desk, on Broadway, when I am semi-asleep at night in our bedroom, struggling to get a good night's rest. There's an overflow of loin energy. It spills out from my pores as if I were a cracked drum of reacting chemicals. I need to work to expend this excess energy in words, stories and books.

At Columbia I am writing and thinking in a new way. My leg still bounces, and my accursed warmth still oozes, but I put fingertips to the keyboard, and words, sentences form. I employ my senses, not analyzing anymore, this nuclear body my vehicle. Robert Olin Butler taught me that. Not the person, but his book, although I bought the book because I met the person and chatted with him. I think Butler-the-Book is mostly right (we should write through our body, which is the one thing we share with every reader). Yet I worry about our visual, glib culture and what it has sacrificed in the name of making books entertainment. Do we not trust any author to have anything to say to us anymore? God is not only dead, but the author as God is dead. We have many bodies writing wonderfully—experiences, perspectives, personal histories—but rarely about the meaning of modern America, or morality, or what should be done. We write with our bodies, but what happened to our minds? We are lost as a culture, and that is entertaining until it matters. Until we have a war. Until China conquers us. Until we realize we have crumpled under our own weight and become another France, without the good wine. It is hard writing in this new way, through the senses only. At least now I am writing, and that's all that matters. I have three pages before my stomach growls and groans. I lug my computer across Broadway to Ollies and pray I do not meet anyone I know.

After a few more hours of semi-writing, I pick up the kids. My three o'clock deadline. I wait at the Bank Street lobby and zero in on the noise around me, the children's chatter, the pleas from the parents. How would I write about that noise? How to put it into words? I practice Butler's suggestions, use my body and its senses as a vehicle for my language. I block everything out; I do not sit on the wooden benches. I stare at the kids and adults walking by, and I focus on their noise, sentence fragments, words and even pleas. I ignore parents whom I know casually, and others just as bodies, faces and legs. My mind is a body that's a mind. They leave me alone, and my head is hot with Butler and my interpretation of Butler. My writing fog has followed me to Bank Street, and I don't want to give it up because I have such precious little time to write, or to think about writing. To further my cause, I need every spare moment. I enjoy myself when I am writing, when my head is at a slow boil, when I am in a scene. I relish this writing physicality, and occasionally it produces a fruit to nourish me. But the real pleasure is this warmth, this over-focus, this becoming lost in words and their sense and scenes beyond the present. This thinking. I hold onto it for a few more minutes, to log a conclusion or revelation before Isaac or Aaron appears and calls me to the present, away from my dream.

But PG shows up. I don't know why he stops in front of me with his practiced smile, why he stands there, smugly awaiting conversation while I stare at the floor. I don't want to talk to him, but I do. Once I was writing a book review in the lobby before my children came out, and I put my hand in his face and said "No" to PG when he approached me. I wanted to finish the work before it escaped my head. He departed in a huff, and didn't talk to me for weeks until I grinned at him again. PG is an artist, and he is also a father who picks up his children. Maybe that's why he wants to be with me, so he doesn't feel alone at Bank Street. I think my concentration attracts him. Why does it not repel him? I am not "trying" to be an artist; I just don't have extra time on my hands as the primary caregiver of my children. I need to work during the spare minutes I have, even as I wait in the lobby for Aaron and Isaac. My piston-leg exhorts me to work. I also don't give a damn what anyone else thinks, nannies and mothers, many of whom believe a solitary man not socializing must be odd. I stay within myself and try to work. At times I am rude to those like PG who don't take the hint. But I am not rude today and I don't know why. Maybe I am getting soft; indeed I am often weak. We chat about stupid things, and I find him full of himself. Yet he is a good father, the best compliment I could give to any man. Isaac greets me with a big hug, and I happily turn my attention to my son. I wave goodbye to PG as Isaac leads me to a kind of freedom.

Isaac and I drop off Aaron at Taekwondo; I will pick Aaron up in an hour. Meanwhile, I walk with Isaac to our apartment, and my back throbs because my laptop weighs about thirty pounds with the books and papers I stuff into its case. Isaac's Hebrew lesson begins, and I take the opportunity to retrieve Aaron at Taekwondo. The Hebrew teacher is fine alone with Isaac, and I trust her. I walk Aaron back to our apartment, another fifteen blocks. I calculated the other day that I walk about four miles each day, for exercise, errands, lessons for the boys, playdates and groceries. Aaron has his Hebrew lesson while Isaac finishes his homework. Our exuberant Hebrew teacher leaves, and the boys finish their homework at their desks, occasionally shouting "Dad! Can you come over here?" or "I don't understand this!" or "Should I do what's due on Thursday too?" I cook dinner and feel like the maid. "Sergio" in Latin means "server," "servant" or "soldier." Yes, I am the servant soldier of this house. When Laura walks in at 7:30 p.m. from her job at the bank, I am slumped on the sofa, having finished washing the dishes and filling the coffee pot for tomorrow morning. The kids watch TV. I am exhausted; my head pulses with pain. Aaron and Isaac will not be asleep before 9:30, their bedtime, and Laura and I will go to bed a few minutes before midnight. The bed is my other sanctum, my deep sleep a rejuvenation, but for what? The Eternal Recurrence of this day?

Should I turn away from my children and Laura? I sometimes think I should, only to get more work done. I have a friend who is gay and a writer. He doesn't have serious attachments for very long; he tells me about a new boyfriend, and then another one. He's in love and then he's not. I have another friend, also a writer, but older. This one dates twenty-one-year-old college students for a few months, women less than half his age, and leaves them, or they leave him, and he's alone again. Then his particular song begins anew. These two writers know each other, and hate each other, but they are actually similar as persons. They think about themselves first and foremost, they have talent and court an entourage, and they obsess about money. They envy me and like Laura and my children. But they also criticize me for focusing too much on my family, and not enough on my writing. I envy their independent lives, their literary production, their oh-so-casual treatment of lovers. First is their work, the promotion of their work and their bragging about their work. They want everybody to pay attention to them. I am like them and I am not. I am passionate about my work, when it is done, when it is successful, but I am also loyal to Laura and my children. That's the price I am willing to pay for my work. Some days I think I am right, and other days I think myself stupid.

I am not saying I cannot be heartless. I know I am often mean. But it pains me and stays with me until I cannot work. I am fulfilled by a love that prompts me to take risks. I write "against the grain," with little care for making money from my words, against the common ethos of writing as entertainment. When your life is wild, I believe you expend needless energy. But what should be the focus? The petty dramas of your life? Or what happens inside your head? For Butler-writing, perhaps, it would be better if I abandoned my love life, à la Gauguin, and wrote about my lusts, conquests, disappointments and travels to the exotic. But what takes you beyond your time? That question gnaws at me. When I read Aristotle's *Nicomachean Ethics* years ago, I remember one thing that rang true: we are moral not just because it is right, but because it feels better, because being immoral consumes so much of your psychic energy and damages your life and the life of your mind. But have we reached a time when morality is pointless, when the life of the mind is a waste of time?

I don't think my writer friends are immoral; it is how they are, and perhaps it works for them. Their lives are indeed entertaining. Yet being a good father and husband works for me. I don't abstractly wish I were different; I'm not sure how I would do that. Yet I envy my friends, in part because their dramas produce more stories publishers want to publish. I have read many of their stories, which are expertly crafted, yet these stories rarely teach me anything, or take me beyond the small world of their personalities. But that's what we often want to read. What has happened to today's reader? What has happened to today's publishers? What will happen to me? I am full of contradictions, and perhaps I am a hypocrite. I can't explain myself half the time. Maybe trying to explain the human being I am, over many different moods and years, amid successes and failures, is a losing proposition. I wish I could write as much, and as well, as I imagine I should write. I wish I could also love and take care of my family. I want to think and write as a loner, as a father, as a husband, as a witness. I wish people would want to read that work, because it would speak to them and point them to a revelation in their lives. Is this too much to ask of writing?

Our apartment on Manhattan's Upper Westside is quiet, and I am writing. Will it be of a quality I can keep? My head, my eyes, ache, yet my mind thinks, and my fingers patter against the keyboard. I will work until my mind is blank, to reach a point where this day is not wasted. Why have I set such a standard for the day? Is there not something wrong with thinking your day is wasted if you do not write good sentences? What kind of strange beings are those who measure themselves this way? I remind myself that words are not life, but symbols. Yet writing is an action, albeit a solitary one (in more ways than one like masturbation), and one in which we are usually writing not about writing but about life.

Do writers, or those who think they are writers, lose themselves in this world of words? I know that words, once I write them and judge them to be worthwhile, remind me of my life, of my thoughts and conclusions from an earlier self. Without words I can't return and easily remember and appreciate my life behind me. I can't see the road I traveled and how I have changed. Without words, I feel as if I never existed. Yet words are such a pale reflection of what I did, what I experienced, who I was when I kissed my children goodnight and heard them recite their prayers and goodnights to Ocistar, who I was when I argued with Laura about how she knew so little about the children's schedules, cutting her to the quick, and then reached beyond myself to be decent, my effort, from nowhere, bringing her back to me and ameliorating her guilt. Words capture a glimpse of these moments, and I fill in the blanks with my mind. Words are the residue that I was there, that I loved my wife, that I kissed my children goodnight, that I sacrificed my life for them. Words are a curse. Life is a curse. Words escape life. Life escapes words. What in God's name am I? How does someone name a God? What is it to name yourself?

Tonight, before I go to sleep, I will take a sleeping pill to pacify my loin energy, to ensure a good rest and to wake up to fight my trap. I need to work. I need to create. I need to never tire of taking my children to school, bringing them back, paying the bills, loving my wife, listening to their complaints and dreams and absurdities. I need to talk to the people in my pickax dreams at the Hudson Valley Writers' Center, and not talk to them as if I want to pickax them, but in a "nice" way, to get what I want, to convince them that quality literary writers, emerging writers, writers of color, need to be our focus, lest they abandon our mission. I need to never have a victim-complex, because once I feel sorry for myself, I won't get anything done. God, with or without a name, won't help me. A good night's sleep will. I need to help myself. I need to have more character, more talent, more savagery. I need the time and focus to accomplish more work to make me exist. Maybe I need to think about Heidegger again, and all his being-towards-death shit, with my death inexorably in front of me to spur me out of my trap. But that is motivation by hate. How long can that last?

Yes, I know I am my trap; perhaps I am inside several traps. I rattle the bars from inside this cage. I stick my arms out and whack passersby. They glare at me and walk away, shaking their heads. Yes, I am trapped, yet once in a while I, or my arm, or spit, or lips, or imagination, escape.

# Apostate of my Literary Family

THE HUDSON VALLEY WRITERS' CENTER HAS BEEN MY LITERARY family for six years. After my first book was published, I was invited to join the board of directors of this small, yet vibrant nonprofit organization in the Westchester suburbs of New York. Like any family, we have argued. Several times I have threatened to quit over what I thought were nonnegotiable issues. Some on the board probably wished I had walked out the door years ago. We have also achieved remarkable success promoting literature in the community. At the height of the Iraq war, two journalists discussed their books about war-torn societies. On another day, Sandy Taylor from Curbstone Press reenergized the room with an off-the-cuff speech on the purpose of literature. Recently Pete Seeger, banjo in hand, chatted in Spanish, sang and jumped to his children's songs and stories, the room jam-packed, just enough space to wiggle, an orange sun setting over the tumultuous swath of water of the Hudson River. I have hated this family, and loved them. I don't know if by the time this essay is published whether I will still be a part of them. But like any family, even when I have left them in my mind, I have come back, because I don't want this literary family to fail. I don't want them to make the wrong choices, because I know they can be better. They have, for better or worse, become a part of me.

With my real family, as with most families related by blood, the perennial issue is love. Is love respect, or is it obedience? Is love independence, or financial support? Can love change? How does it change? Is love acceptance without questions or challenges? Is love, at a certain point, neglect? Or can love be nostalgia for what once was? Can love, finally, be the hate that comes from self-recognition, from criticism that truly stings, from a pointed word by one who knows you as well as you know yourself?

Within my literary family, the perennial question has been about literature. Why does the Hudson Valley Writers' Center exist as an organization? What is its purpose? What is its soul? This question is in one way similar to the question a real family asks of itself. When a real family asks what is love, it is also asking, in a way, why this family should matter.

About five years ago, board members of the Hudson Valley Writers' Center debated whether we might become an elitist literary organization if we removed certain programs not directly literary. Besides classes and workshops, a reading series with established and emerging writers and Slapering Hol Press, our poetry imprint, we also had smaller programs to help disadvantaged children in schools and to train teachers in writing. At the root of our debate were assumptions about what constitutes literature.

I wondered why some would even relate the literary with elitism, unless they harbored a strange view of what literature is, or should be. I have written about *los de abajo* from El

Paso—janitors, maids, farmworkers—because I grew up poor, and because I believe I understand this community. So I found it strange people would say literature is necessarily elitist.

I believe you can craft good stories about social change, difficult questions of class, the morality and minds of the poor, which too often are overlooked in stereotypes of the disenfranchised. I certainly don't write elitist literature in any sense. I always assumed writing was, indeed, outreach to the poor, to those voices I grew up with who were not heard. I certainly never felt guilty about my writing.

I think someone who thinks writers and their literature are elitist must have a certain view of good literature or literature with a capital L that must be challenged. Literature is not just about unique images with beautiful words. It is not an activity somehow divorced from raw moral conflicts, or the life of the poor, or life-and-death questions which we all face. When you divorce writing from these concerns, then of course, literature becomes a meaningless, self-referential Art for and about the elite. But that is a peculiar view of literature, which I would not call Literature. James Joyce, for example, wrote about a profound and ordinary day in the life of the Irish poor, in *Ulysses*. William Faulkner wrote about the moral conflicts between blacks and whites in the South. Jamaica Kincaid writes about working-class immigrants, the uneasy relationships with their parents and the well-to-do culture of the Northeast.

I found it very natural to think our outreach at the Hudson Valley Writers' Center should be accomplished *through* writing, with our classes and workshops, readings series and publications, and not as something separate from the main activities of writing itself. Only if you see literature as divorced from the common man and his concerns will you become worried that a focus on writing itself will become elitist. I would argue that you have a peculiar definition of literature if you think that way.

A corollary of this peculiar view of literature, as an ornament, and not a social force in itself, is that you will assume the poor will not be able to produce, or even appreciate, proper Literature. If Literature is only about the proper use of English, its prettiness, unique and astonishing sentence constructions, then someone writing about, say, characters from Ysleta or Spanish Harlem is not writing Literature at all. Let's just call it (patronizingly) Ethnic Literature (which separates it from real Literature, or American Literature). This ornamental view of Literature will assume the disenfranchised are not interested in real Literature or excellent writing. Again, these assumptions should be challenged, and refuted.

Poor people discuss ideas. Poor people read. Poor people want to learn. Poor people can appreciate good stories. They want to write well and have their voices heard. Everybody enjoys good writing. We also need to get rid of the stereotypes that *los de abajo* do not think and do not debate moral issues. They do. The problem is that too often they are ignored.

Sometimes even Chicanos themselves think this way about their community. How many times have I read, or heard, a Chicano writer claim that he or she writes only about "life as it is," which presumably excludes writing about ideas, or philosophical and moral questions. The assumption is that authentic Chicanos do not think, that the only stories that matter to our community are stories about picking grapes, or gang warfare, or the racism which we do face everyday, subtle as well as brutal. Of course, much of our community is poor, and can barely survive day-to-day. Yet even *los de abajo* think; even they ponder, intelligently and profoundly, the questions that have plagued the higher echelons of society. The poor may even have something to teach the rich about morality, trust, relationships, what is right. Of course, not all Chicanos are poor, not all have fathers or mothers who were farmworkers. That simple fact could never be stated by anyone of goodwill in order to demean those who harvest the grapes and corn and strawberries for Fairway Market in New York. That fact is stated to broaden the conception of what a Chicano is, within our community, and without. That fact is stated because this Chicano is proud of who he is and does not suffer from a form of self-racism which excludes achievement or success as being part of the definition of who he is, or can be. It is difficult enough when the rich suburbs of New York City possess a stereotypical image of who you are, which you should fight to change. But let's not do it to ourselves too. There is no guilt in the heart when you know what you do is true.

How did a Chicano from the Mexican-American border of El Paso, Texas, become a board member of the Hudson Valley Writers' Center in Westchester? How did these people ever become part of my literary family? These questions have haunted me ever since I joined the Writers' Center and its debates six years ago. It is an understatement to say I felt out of place. In the beginning, I thought some fellow board members were strange characters come to life from my dreams: John Houseman qua Charles W. Kingsfield, Jr., Ichabod Crane from "The Legend of Sleepy Hollow," Mrs. Robinson from "The Graduate" and the smiley Anglo librarian who could barely conceal her disdain whenever little brown faces attempted to check out books from "her library" in downtown El Paso. Over time, I did not see my colleagues as caricatures anymore, but as complex human beings, some with whom I disagreed, and others who inspired me. Did their view of who a Chicano was, or could be, ever change? I don't know. I know I was the first Mexican American some had known well. For many years, I was the only minority on the board of directors.

I was invited to be part of the Writers' Center, because I had written a well-received first book, but more importantly, because Don and Margo Stever, who founded the Writers' Center in 1988, knew me from my years as a Harvard undergraduate. The summer of my sophomore year I had not returned to El Paso, but had instead set my sights on Washington, D.C. Many fellow Gov majors applied for summer internships, and I had become confident enough about succeeding at Harvard that I wanted to try what the more ambitious students did for the summer. But I did not go about it the same way. By chance, after glancing at a bulletin board at Harvard's Kennedy School of Government, I called a Maryland number and immediately found a place to stay with Harvard alumnus and poet Margo Stever and her husband Don, an environmental lawyer. Then I contacted my congressman, Richard White of El Paso, and told his staff I was searching for a summer internship in the capitol. His office, after weeks of delay, finally responded definitively in late April. Their internships had been awarded to students from SMU and Texas Tech, presumably to students much better connected politically than anyone from Ysleta. I told them I was coming to Washington anyway. A manager in White's office promised me "something."

That undergraduate summer my reward from Representative White and his office was a job in the factory-like windowless basement of the U.S. House of Representatives. The mailroom. Massive, clackety machines printed, folded and sorted the junk newsletters and circulars congressmen stuff in mailboxes across the country. I was the only "white kid" in the basement, and for the first few days I felt deeply ashamed. My Harvard friends bragged about attending hearings, briefing senators, writing policy papers and partying at Georgetown barbecues. I sweated in the hot basement, loaded machine after machine with paper, boxed and carted off endless piles of propaganda. At first, the black workers looked at me as if I were a weird duck in a tie. For weeks, I lied to the Stevers.

That summer, I donned an oxford shirt and tie, said goodbye to Don in his maroon Volvo in front of the Cannon Office Building, yanked my tie off in the bathroom and slipped into a T-shirt. When I emerged from my hellhole at the end of the day to meet Don at the Justice Department for a ride home to Chevy Chase, Maryland, I again wore my white-collar disguise. During this summer in Washington, I had often felt like a phony, but I survived.

Now at the Hudson Valley Writers' Center I was not an undergraduate anymore, but a writer. I taught a fiction workshop at Yale during the summer I was married with two children and lived in Manhattan. But in strange Westchester, I still felt I did not belong. Sometimes a few choice individuals made it a point to treat me as if I did not belong, or belonged only as a token minority. I remember, literally at my first board meeting, one woman came over to tell me what she wanted me to do as a board member. She ordered me to focus on "neighborhood outreach to the Latino community," and I responded by saying, yes, I wanted to reach out to Latino writers in particular, but I also knew many great writers who weren't Latino. I was also interested in the financial aspects of the Writers' Center. (I had been, for a short period, an economist). She retorted by saying that wasn't what she meant, or what she wanted me to do. I ended the conversation by telling her I would find my own way, and I did. The Stevers felt I belonged, and that's what mattered to me.

I contrast that first board meeting at the Hudson Valley Writers' Center with my first board meeting at Curbstone Press, where many years later I also joined their board of directors. Sandy Taylor asked what I was interested in, and listened. Then he proceeded to give me not only copies of Curbstone's financial accounts, with brokers and banks, but copies of his own personal accounts. Sandy asked me to review the documents and give him advice on what to do. The amount and depth of immediate trust from Sandy Taylor astonished me, and forever made me indebted to him and Curbstone Press. That simple act encouraged me to feel immediately like part of the Curbstone family. But at the Writers' Center achieving a sense of belonging took time, effort and pain, the pain of breaking barriers and changing people's initial perceptions of who I was, or could be.

I also have to admit I changed during my first 6 years on the board of the Writers' Center. That was also a factor in my participating in their debates as a true colleague and not just as a token or somebody's underling. Being part of any family is always a two-way street. I changed by being less of a bomb-thrower, or loose cannon (take your pick of a military metaphor), and evolved into an effective board member who could change the organization from within. I could still criticize it severely, but without *ad hominem* attacks or friendship-ending clashes. The primary reason I changed was that I wanted to be effective; I wanted to get things done. You don't get things done, in any organization, if you alienate your potential allies. I found that out the hard way. I also adapted because I learned from my nemesis. I noticed how her outward geniality and apparent agreement with you and others, often masked virulent dislike for anyone who questioned her, and camouflaged her manipulation to get her way. I did not want to become like my nemesis, but I understood I would probably lose the board's support if my tone was wrong, acerbic or mean.

I know some on the board of the Hudson Valley Writers' Center believed I was simply a "hot-headed Latino." But my initial attitude was a response to being disrespected, to having to endlessly explain issues of literature to those who were not writers, to justifying the importance of Latino writers to those who did not read much literature (Latino or otherwise). True, I possess a streak of righteousness that has always valued being right at the expense of being liked. Yet it is hard not to react angrily when someone criticizes your very right to be at the decision-making table. But you must react with words and argument, and by describing the kind of attack you face. You must convince others how this attack conceals a power-play, prejudice, incompetence or ignorance.

I wonder if the most important lesson I learned at the Hudson Valley Writers' Center is whether, and when, to sublimate or redirect instinctual personal reactions into socially acceptable points of view and arguments. Perhaps this is a function of any family, to convert its members into socially functional human beings. Writers in particular, I have noticed over the years, have a difficult time being other than ridiculously adamant about their literary opinions. We spend too much time alone, the nature of a writer's work. We often suffer alone with our fears and insecurities, and bolster ourselves with chutzpah. The best writers take a purposeful step, or two, or twenty, away from society, to better tell the stories that need to be told, to adopt overlooked perspectives, to reveal to the many what they have refused to see for themselves. Because of these intrinsic realities of the literary life, many writers are not easily part of any family. Some writers live schizophrenic lives, at once social and solitary. Others learn to be effective for a while, in board meetings which are literally and figuratively thousands of miles from where they began. Still other writers join a literary family, and for a while maintain an uneasy existence within this family. Sooner or later they may question whether the knowledge and success gained have not dulled the knife of truth that once shaped the purpose of their writing.

A few days ago, I sat at the Sleepy Hollow Country Club with other members of the board of directors of the Hudson Valley Writers' Center. We were having a board retreat to discuss, again, the future of the Writers' Center and why we should exist. What struck me most about the meeting was not the discussion we had—which was at times substantive—but the setting. The dark, paneled walls of wood were lined with portraits of old white men, dignified, important, comfortably rich. Not a single woman was on those walls, not one Latino, not one African American. The waiters—who served us coffee and pastries and our lunch after we selected it from an elaborate menu—wore crisp, black and white outfits, their backs stiff and straight. They projected the studied formality expected of them. I thought about Sartre's description of a waiter in *Being and Nothingness*: the waiter, who plays the role of a waiter and so denies being a waiter by his very effort to play the role of a waiter. I asked a waiter if she knew Spanish, because I thought I had detected a Spanish accent as she asked about my order. I did not like the distance between us, because I have always been uncomfortable with someone serving me. I knew others in that boardroom were quite comfortable with being served by fancy waiters. The woman who took my order did not know Spanish. She was a recent immigrant from Eastern Europe. She smiled at me and moved to the next person. Was I, like the waiter in Sartre's example, also in "bad faith" at this board meeting at the Sleepy Hollow Country Club?

I point out the setting of our retreat not because I would have preferred to have our meeting at a loud, corner *taquería* in Spanish Harlem, but because setting does affect culture, discourse, what is important and what is thought to be obviously true. There were good reasons to have our retreat at the Sleepy Hollow Country Club. A board member had easily acquired permission to use the boardroom, and the room possessed a table big enough to have everybody sit around it. But imagine if we had had our meeting at a library, surrounded by the faces of inspiring writers—Joyce, Faulkner, Baldwin, Hurston, Cisneros, Roth, Updike, Gilb, Oates—rather than by the eerie portraits of old, rich white men? Would our discussions have been not about money, how to raise it and how to tailor our programs to "available corporate funding," but about how we choose the best emerging writers to invite to our center? Would we have instead discussed how we put good writers who are also good teachers in a position to evaluate our teachers to keep the high quality of our classes intact? Would we have focused on how we keep this Writers' Center a place for working writers, not just a club for wealthy people who dabble in writing?

I did not feel as if I did not belong at the table anymore, so that wasn't the root of my Sartrean "bad faith," or whatever was bothering me. I knew I had over the years contributed substantially to the Writers' Center, from improving our finances, drafting and passing an Investment Policy Statement to invest our fledgling endowment, leading the drive to rationalize the pricing structure of our classes, to bringing in writers like Jamaica Kincaid, Dagoberto Gilb, Richard Price, Ernesto Quiñonez, Ilan Stavans and great new poets like María Meléndez and Rigoberto González. I organized many memorable readings, including a reading on war with Bill Berkeley and Peter Maass, and another to honor the University of Arizona Press' Camino Del Sol series for Latino writers. I even helped the talented playwright, Brighde Mullins, publish her first book of poetry with our Slapering Hol Press. So I knew I belonged at the table; I had paid my dues. Maybe the question on my mind was whether I should stay at this table and enter another era of fighting battles to make working writers relevant. I had fought long to keep the focus away from money and fame, and on good writing, the social importance of literature and edgy stories that give voice to who has been silenced in American culture.

Perhaps I did not belong in this setting anymore, at the Sleepy Hollow Country Club and the Hudson Valley Writers'

Center, not because I was fighting for legitimacy, but because I was unsure if they would keep changing. I was tired of being the catalyst to make them change. At that moment, I did not want to counter, yet again, the assumptions about literature that routinely swirl within the hallowed enclaves of Westchester's elite. I did not want to fight against those who spent a few weekends a month as "writers." I did not want to educate others of good conscience also in the room about why literature that might not be popular might contain the best writing. What would be the point in deflating another pontificator who, having never read a word from a particular writer, would nevertheless attempt to undermine an invitation to a unique wordsmith? Setting affects culture; setting affects what questions are discussed, and how. Setting affects what's on the agenda, and what and who are not. Was this the right setting for me? I did not know anymore.

The most basic lesson I have learned from my experiences with this Westchester literary family is that rich people assume they are right in large part because they are rich. In retrospect, maybe that should have been obvious to me, but it wasn't. I did discover fascinating characteristics among those who have inherited their wealth through their families and by divorces. These inherited rich are invariably well-spoken and polished, and often rise to leadership positions in nonprofits even though they may be making awful decisions for their organizations. The inherited rich assume their importance despite evidence to the contrary. The reason, of course, anyone listens to the inherited rich of Westchester, or Hastings-on-Hudson, is that they have money, and they give away a little bit of it every year. But their cocoon of money protects them from the truth, from work, from not only people being honest with them, but from their being honest with themselves. Rich people don't have to have a life-and-death relationship with the truth and its questions; they can ignore the truth and still thrive materially. I am not surprised many of them understand literature only as an ornament. Life is an ornament to them, relationships are ornaments, their "work" is but a flimsy, pretty ornament meant to momentarily thrill and capture attention. Why didn't I reread my F. Scott Fitzgerald sooner? I might have saved myself some time.

As I sat at the Sleepy Hollow Country Club and glanced at the portraits on the wall, I did not know what, if any, relationship I should continue with the Hudson Valley Writers' Center. I didn't think it was a mistake to join them. I didn't think it was a mistake to help them. I helped many writers get into the door of the Writers' Center, writers whose voices would otherwise have never been heard in Sleepy Hollow. I was inspired by some members on our board, who despite their "rich disadvantage," would still seek out the truth for its own sake even against their first inclinations. Others, unfortunately, never escaped their cocoons of wealth and became characters trapped in their fantasy worlds of self-importance, false friendships and eccentricity-qua-meaning-in-life. I did not set out to reform anybody. But I believed they learned from me as much as I learned from them. Would staying with this family be a mistake? Perhaps it would be like trying to pretend that I was one of them, and that I was like them in more ways than one, at the same time that I was denying trying to be like them, and denying who I was and where I should be. I don't think I could live like that.

I have a poet-friend, Rigoberto, who is a member of Con Tinta, an advocacy group of Latino writers, and I was having lunch with him at Artie's. I mentioned I would be glad to offer my co-op's private party room for the Con Tinta party at the Associated Writing Program's conference in New York next year. We were a few blocks from my apartment building on

Manhattan's Upper Westside, and I wanted Rigo to see the party room and decide if it might be suitable for Con Tinta. We strolled into the two-story lobby of polished marble and steel, the nattily dressed doorman greeted me by name, and I asked our concierge for the keys to the private party room. I showed Rigoberto the room, big enough to hold small weddings and bar mitzvahs, a carpeted two-story duplex with its own kitchen and bathrooms, and a view of the co-op's sun deck and health club. As we walked out to Broadway again, Rigoberto whispered to me, "Are you sure they'll let a bunch of Chicanos in here?" I turned to him, surprised by his comment, and looked into his eyes to see if he was joking, and he wasn't. "Rigo, stop thinking that way. You belong here. You should assume you belong here. We all belong here. That's one of our biggest problems. We do these *pendejadas* to ourselves even before others do them to us."

Is it better to assume, as one writer suggested to me after I mentioned this incident at a literary forum in El Paso, that Mexican Americans do not belong at places like the Hudson Valley Writers' Center? "We do not belong, we have never belonged and we shouldn't pretend to belong in the power structure." Or is it better to think, as Benjamin Saenz retorted after he joined our debate on the dais, that "it's so easy to throw rocks, or pebbles, from the outside. It's much harder to make organizations change, to be the agent of change from within." In El Paso, I responded to these writers only by saying it was a lonely fight. I told them that I often wanted to quit. But I did feel a responsibility as "a gatekeeper," as Saenz called me. At the moment, I still wanted to keep bringing good writers to Westchester, particularly good Latino writers, and to fight for my literary causes as an outsider inside the boardroom.

But was I really an outsider anymore? What kind of insider-outsider was I, after six years on the board of directors? More importantly, what standards should I uphold, as an insider-outsider, to maintain my center of gravity in the literary world? This, I believed, was the gist of the issue. Competing, contradictory and ever-shifting standards. On the one hand, some people thought, like a *New York Times* book editor who recently visited El Paso, that "Chicano literature does not influence American literature." The assumption is that Mexican-American literature is not, nor will it ever be, part of great American literature. The belief is that a group whose ancestors often grew up speaking Spanish, or who are comfortable in a linguistic hodgepodge called Spanglish, would never master the skills to write great literature in English. On the other hand, others are like my writer-friend in El Paso, who trumpeted our outsider status, pointedly reminded me of the racism we faced as Chicanos and implicitly criticized my belonging to a mainstream organization as naïve and stupid. The assumption here is that Chicanos will never be included, nor should they try to be included, in traditional literary circles. The belief is that we shouldn't even attempt to emulate Shakespearean English, or whatever literary standard vaguely exists in the minds of the American literary elite. Perhaps the assumption is also that we, Chicanos, should stay within our community and simply help each other out.

My view has been practical and, I hope, thoughtful, and does not easily fall into either camp. *The New York Times* editor lived in New York, one of the last places that will appreciate how the United States will inexorably be facing south, toward Latin America, culturally, politically and ethnically. Europe is the past. The editor also adhered to an outmoded sense of English as a language affixed in some musty tome, or time, and not as a language shaped by other languages, including Spanish, and by a variety of practitioners beyond Oxford, Cambridge, the Ivy League or the cognoscenti of *The New York Times*.

My El Paso friend, the proud outsider, used the ethnic discrimination and cultural arrogance we indeed face as Chicanos and Latinos, as barriers to prevent hard comparisons of our literary work with the world beyond. Our stories and poems have to compete with the excellence of craftsmanship in the greater literary world, yet if this world is open-minded enough, it will recognize that our stories should change what the standard should be for great American literature. My friend probably did not believe those in the Hudson Valley Writers' Center would ever be open-minded enough. Perhaps he thought the Westchester crowd would stick with only the culturally familiar standards, and would always relegate any-thing written by a Chicano (with a pat on the head) to the desolate corner of Ethnic Literature. I would have told my friend that, yes, there are those who will never change. But there are others who do listen, and over time, change their perspectives about what is great literature and who should be included as worthy American writers. But it takes work. Lone-ly, thankless work. Also, you are more likely to do this work if you possess a strong sense of self, beyond what others think of you, or expect from you.

To appreciate where I stand, in El Paso or New York, I wish everyone could see my character. It is somewhere between white and black, let's say brown, like mud, the most complex color of colors. I am a mestizo, in between, searching, ques-tioning. I am an insider-outsider, and I believe we belong in places like the Hudson Valley Writers' Center. But my sense of belonging has never been to be too comfortable with any place, to forget to ask the questions that silently hang in the air, to refuse to challenge the happy conclusions of those who prefer conformity over thinking. I do wish everyone could see my character like a color, the mettle of what is inside of me. I wish they could see my work, which is neither good or bad, not elitist or Chicano, but brown, the color of work. It is within this middle earth where the world reverberates with life.

# This Wicked Patch of Dust

I AM IN THE MIDDLE OF A FIGHT WITH MY FATHER. ONE THAT has lasted almost a year. I have argued with my father many times, as a child and as a teenager. Years ago I almost punched him in our kitchen in Ysleta, in a blinding anger over something I cannot now remember. But this year, I am an adult, forty-five years old, and my father is old and frail. He suffers with back problems that prevent him from walking more than ten feet at a time. Thousands of miles separate us. He lives in Ysleta, in the adobe house where I was born, on the Mexican-American border of El Paso, Texas. I live in New York City, making my life as a writer within the murky battlegrounds of literary craftsmanship and taste, the chronically ill book industry and fledgling, nonprofit literary organizations, the politics of which turn my stomach. My father fought to survive in the United States as a Mexican immigrant without great skills in English, never physically or culturally straying far from his Mexican homeland. I fight to be an independent, even philosophical Chicano writer in New York City, New

Orleans and Washington, D.C. We are both men in exile in strange lands, stubborn, lonely even when surrounded by family, and mean. My father's mother died when he was ten years old, and that trauma has forever shaped how he views women (on a pedestal, and yet servile), and how he sees himself (as a survivor, damaged, but gritty and unbeaten). I am my mother's son, in love with words and numbers, curious about politics and willing to sacrifice for my family, even at the expense of what is best for me. The fight I had with my father last Christmas, I fear, has irreparably damaged our relationship like no other fight before it. Soon he will be dead.

Our argument began, as so many family arguments do, over a problem trivial and stupid. My wife Laura and I, and our two sons, Aaron (11) and Isaac (8), always visit El Paso for one week over Christmas. Over the past two years, my father's health has deteriorated. He has diabetes and was fighting an infection on his toe, which of course he knew about for months, but preferred not to mention it to anybody, including my mother, until the toe developed a rancid hole the size of a nickel. Just before our trip to El Paso, my father had also injured his back, working on the apartments he owns in downtown El Paso, apartments I have begged him to sell, to no avail. There are endless hassles with unruly tenants, their overdue rents and the chores of upkeep, from fixing boilers, to weeding the yard, to shutting off the water at midnight to stop a rusty pipe's waterfall from the second to the first floor. A week before we arrived for our Christmas visit, my father, with his bad back, refused to patiently sit in a chair at a Wal-Mart to wait for my mother while she purchased medicines for him. According to him, she took too long, and he began to wander the Wal-Mart aisles in search of my mother. I can imagine his haggard brown face impatient, his small green eyes desperate, his legs spindly, yet shuffling underneath him. My father did not get too far. He slipped, or tripped and fractured his shoulder in the store. Bad back, broken shoulder, infected toe. That's how we found him at Christmastime.

During our visit, my father, Rodolfo, sat on the velvety red couch in our living room, alone, sometimes watching TV, dozing. My mother checked on him repeatedly and asked him what he needed, and drove him to doctor appointments. One morning I walked into the kitchen and heard him yell to my mother that the DVD player did not work, that the kids had broken it. I marched into the living room.

"What happened to the DVD player?" I kneeled and tried to turn the machine on, my father behind me, sitting on the velvety red couch, his walker next to him. His short grayish hair was nearly at a crew-cut, and he wore a faded red sweatshirt. I thought he had lost some weight.

"Last night the kids wanted to watch a movie and I think they broke it."

"But they didn't use this DVD player. I put them on the laptop in Rudy's room. They didn't touch it. They watched their movie on my laptop." The machine still wouldn't turn on, and I jiggled the nest of electrical cords behind their stereo, DVD player, clock and TV. The surge protector's light glimmered neon red.

"I saw them searching for something, looking behind the machines."

"But they didn't touch it. I told you, they watched their movie somewhere else." My father was angry I had contradicted him, but I didn't care. I was angry too. I knew he was wrong, and my guess was that Aaron or Isaac had tried to turn on the DVD player in the living room. When it didn't work, they asked me to play "Cheaper By The Dozen" on the laptop.

"Caleb and Joshua do the same thing. *Los niños de* Oscar come over here, destroy things and Lee Ann and Oscar never tell them anything," he said in a breathless, exasperated retort, as if his cracking emotion, and what it portended, should end the issue. My father was talking about my brother's kids, but again I knew my father was wrong. My brother is as tough on his kids as I am on my kids: if they break something, they pick it up and fix it, or pay for it. We do not spoil our children. I personally hate the over-involved, over-protective Upper Westside parents who raise children as if they can do no wrong, and end up with foul-mouthed brats, undisciplined wildings or irresponsible conceits. I have seen these family dynamics so many times. The teachers know exactly who these kids are and why so much time is wasted fixing behavioral problems in the classroom that should have been fixed at home. My kids are not like that; my brother's kids are not like that. As Aaron says to me, "My friends think you are the toughest dad at Bank Street." This is not meant as a compliment.

"Aaron and Isaac did not break this DVD. I told you, they didn't touch it."

"I saw them fiddling with this machine and now it doesn't work."

I ordered Aaron and Isaac into the living room. "*Abuelito* says you broke the DVD player. He is blaming you for breaking it. Have you been playing with this machine?" My children repeated what I had said, that the machine didn't work, that they watched their movie on my laptop the night before. They marched out of the living room, and I heard Laura in the kitchen urge them outside with Running Bear.

"Why are you blaming them for breaking the DVD? You always want to blame someone. Maybe you broke it yourself." I was angry at my father, the blood in my heart boiling. I didn't care how he reacted; I knew he was wrong. I felt a red and black emotion rising in my chest to my face, a misty, poisonous cloud. I knew my father was weak. I also knew he wouldn't stand to be contradicted, even in the face of facts, witnesses or logic. Nothing mattered, except his opinion. That had always been the way with him. I stood up and faced him.

"Of course they're going to tell you what you want to hear. You don't know how to raise your own children."

"What are you talking about? They didn't touch your stupid DVD player. You just can't admit you're wrong, and you are wrong. Why don't you have the guts to admit you're wrong?"

"Get the hell out of here! Who the hell do you think you are talking to me that way!"

I walked up to him, and put my face in front of his face. "You are just a stupid old man. You can't even admit you are wrong. You blame children when maybe you should be blaming yourself. *Levántate, pues,* if you want to do something about it!" My father struggled to get off the couch, like a crab on its back helplessly waving its spindly legs in the air, but he could not stand up. His body had betrayed him, even if his mind and voice had not. I had never used such words against him. His face was contorted with a vengeful anger. He yelled to my mother to tell her what I had said in my impertinence, to tell her to take him away from me, to witness this spectacle in the living room, of a father and son breaking away from each other.

"You're the idiot! You don't know what you are talking about! I said I 'thought' they broke it. You're the liar! How dare you talk to me that way! Did you hear what he said to me?" my father yelled, searching for my mother over my shoulder. My mother was not there yet.

"If you had any decency, you talk about following God, and about going to church, but you can't admit you're wrong. Why can't you say 'I made a mistake'?"

"Don't ever talk to me again! Idiot! You are the stupid one!"

"Get up off the couch and do something about it then! I'm sick and tired of it!" I roared at him, only two feet away. My mother finally rushed from the kitchen and stood between us.

"You rule this house like a dictator! Everything you say is law! But you don't even know what you're doing anymore! You don't have the courage to say you're wrong! You can't even get up off the couch! You are a stupid, bitter old man! The sooner you die, the better for all of us!"

"Sergio, ¡ay Dios! In the name of God, please stop!" my mother beseeched me. I stomped out of the living room.

I immediately threatened to cut short our vacation, to Laura, to anybody who would listen, but I only clenched my fists. Laura rolled her eyes at me and left me alone. I paced in the bedroom like a panther that has been denied a meal, wanting, truly, to kill my father. For blaming my children for something they did not do; for lying to himself and others; for his fake power and ridiculous pronouncements (over which my brothers routinely roll their eyes behind his back, yet never dare say a word to his face); for forcing my mother to serve him like a servant at each meal and treating her like a slave; for not getting her a nicer house with a garden, in a better neighborhood, even though he could have easily afforded it, and she had desperately wanted it for years; for his mule-headed stubbornness, beyond reason or logic or facts; for his homophobia and self-satisfied Catholicism, not truly spiritual like my mother's, but convenient, fearful and punitive; for once kicking me and my brothers in our room, entranced by a murderous rage, after we had broken something or had said something, and he had returned from work exhausted and on the edge, and my mother had had enough of three wild boys who wouldn't listen, who would chuckle and refuse to do what she asked them to do, yes, for kicking our backs and our stomachs, his face in a seizure, his power unquestioned, his brutal methods, this red anger that left our home quiet as a forsaken cemetery for hours, with only our whimpers interrupting the night.

After our argument, I avoided the living room and did not see my father for the last three days of our Christmas vacation in El Paso. He mostly stayed in his room, but occasionally he returned to his velvety red couch to watch television. The day before we left, at the urging of my mother, I walked to the living room to apologize to my father, for my cruel words and anger, for disrespecting him. I did it for my mother. I did not think I was wrong. I did think I was harsh, and I knew I was mean. But I did not think I was wrong. I apologized as a lie, to make him feel better, but mostly to stop my mother from her self-imposed agony over the conflicts in our family, to stop her emotional distress and incessant praying, her sudden, tearful outbursts at the kitchen table. I did not want to hurt her, I did not want her to suffer, and so I apologized to him, as meekly as I could, as he would have expected, as I had done as a child. And he rejected it, rejected me, from his velvety red couch. I persisted and apologized again, repeating I was sorry for what I said and that I hadn't really meant those words. He told me to leave the room and never talk to him again.

The next day, an hour before our departure, I approached him in the living room again, and tried to hug him goodbye. My father yanked his head away and told me to leave him alone. We left El Paso for New York, and have not returned since that day.

I have thought about what was said, and why it was said, for weeks and then months after the argument with my father. My mother and I still talk by phone every week, and our conversations are invariably about the argument. She has reiterated my father is sick, vulnerable and in pain. In his condition, she says, my father has become irrational and bitter about what has happened to him. It is not pleasant getting old, she tells me, and different people handle it in different ways. My mother Bertha reminds me of how my beloved *abuelitos* died, Doña Dolores and Don José Rivero, her parents. My mother

cared for them when they could not live alone in the apartment my father had provided free for decades, the best one in
the two buildings my father owns. When my *abuelitos* were in
their eighties, my mother moved them into a small apartment
my parents built in the backyard of our house in Ysleta.
Doña Dolores slowly lost her mental faculties, and my
mother soon washed her like a baby in the bathtub. My mother recounted how Doña Lola would unleash the strangest
rebukes, unconnected to anything happening around them or
would suddenly remember her own mother (my great-grand-
mother) as if my *abuelita* had reverted to childhood. Doña
Dolores died in our backyard apartment one morning, having
never awoken from the night before, at peace, surrounded by
her family.

My grandfather, Don José, had been a genial old man,
quick with a laugh or a toothy grin. He loved recounting corny
jokes and flashing his mishmash of golden teeth. Once he
lived in our backyard apartment, after my grandmother had
died next to him in her sleep, Don José became more somber
for a few months. Soon enough he reverted to his easygoing,
amiable self. He spent many mornings asleep on our porch.
Prince, our German Shepherd before Running Bear, dozed at
his feet, the sunlight agleam on my grandfather's chocolatey
brown bald head, the desert wind lazily rustling through the
waxy thick mulberry leaves. My grandfather lived more years
than my grandmother, and never lost his mind. Don José possessed a strong body and an unbelievable grip, his hands like
an eagle's talons. He had been a copper miner in Arizona, a
chicken hauler in Texas and a gardener in Socorro, the rural
hamlet next to Ysleta. One morning my mother discovered
her father hunched against the wall of his bed, as if Don José
had tried to get up during the middle of the night but had
remained frozen mid-cough. As my mother looked closer in
the dim morning light, she noticed blood against the wall,

blood on his chest, a thick clot of blood stuck in his mouth like a wad of cotton. My grandfather was dead. Don José also died surrounded by his family, not peacefully in his sleep, but struggling to stay alive, yet also loved by his children. In other phone conversations I have had with my mother, she has upbraided me, saying I should never have spoken to my father that way. My tone was inappropriate, and he didn't deserve my harsh words, even if he had been wrong about the DVD player. "Wait until you get old, and Aaron and Isaac start contradicting you, start criticizing you, and you will see how you react. You'll be angry, you'll still see them as children who should know their place, even though they will be adults, and with their own families, and their own successes and failures. You may even know in your heart you are wrong, but your pride will not let you admit it, your anger about your body, your shock at seeing the shell of a man you have become. Just wait and you will see. No son should speak to a father the way you spoke to your father, even if the father is wrong. You have no right to judge him. Only *Dios Nuestro Señor* will judge your *papá.*"

Indeed, my mother has reminded me that he was a good father despite his failures of character, his temper, his stubbornness (which she points out I inherited). I may have inherited my stubbornness from both Doña Dolores and my father. I am like both of them in many ways, and in other ways I am not. My mother reminds me of the time my father spent with us as boys, how he taught us to work hard to scratch a living out of this godforsaken desert (although she does not use the word "godforsaken" to describe Ysleta, but instead calls it *"este maldito terregal,"* or this wicked patch of dust). She tells me about the sacrifices my father made for our family, working every day of his adult life as a draftsman for demanding bosses, working construction on weekends at *los departamentos,* suffering with diabetes since he was forty years old. She reminds

me that my father's mother died when he was just a *niño*, only
to be replaced with a stepmother who hated the youngest son
of Santiago Troncoso. My father's father, according to family
lore, did not love him and sent him into the world, at eighteen, with but twenty dollars and a handshake. My mother
reminds me we were not easy children, that I in particular was
always *terco* and *enojado* and *duro*. My mother tells me it was a
struggle for them too, to have such a bright son who was stubborn beyond belief. "As a toddler, you even argued one day
when your *abuelita* walked by you, and you lost your balance
and fell down. You blamed her. '*Atumbastes*,' you accused her,
in your baby Spanish. Doña Lola shot back, arguing you fell by
yourself, that the mere swish of air had caused you to fall, and
that you were just a *mentiroso*, a little liar. '¡*Atumbastes!*
¡*Atumbastes!*' you yelled back. You wouldn't back down.
Everyone was afraid of her, but you wouldn't back down. You
were just a baby, and you were arguing and standing toe-to-toe
against *la revolucionaria*, Doña Dolores Rivero." Over the
phone—I have unlimited long-distance service—my mother
has also reminded me of the lime-green bookshelves my father
created in my room in grade school, the dozens of posters he
hand-lettered for my candidacy for Sophomore Class President at Ysleta High School and the countless checks he sent
to me for Harvard, Yale, Europe, the Blairstown Summer
School for Journalism. "He was a good father and we did what
we could. Just look at how all of you turned out. Each of you
is successful and married and has a good career. Why do you
think you are the person you are today?"

After listening to my mother, I reached out to my father
again. From New York, I called El Paso every week, just as I
have for years. Sometimes he picked up the phone. For three
months after our Christmas argument, whenever my father
would pick up the phone, I would hang up. I didn't want to
talk to him; I was still angry. I didn't know how he would

react, and I didn't want to find out. Maybe I was scared or embarrassed. I certainly didn't want to be humiliated or rejected again; I didn't think I deserved it. Once or twice when I hung up, I immediately heard my cell phone ring, and the call came from my father's cell phone. But no message was ever left. Was he reaching out to me too, or did my father know I was hanging up on him and wanted to let me know that he knew? I don't know why we are like that; I don't know why men are like that. When I called El Paso, my mother would just as often pick up the phone as my father. That's when I spoke to her. I discovered my father went to sleep early (El Paso time), and I could call around 11 p.m. (New York time: two hours later) and get my mother.

But one weekend, maybe in March or April, I called and my father answered and I said hello. Immediately he said he would get my mother and, without saying another word, handed the phone to her. This happened repeatedly until about a month later, in May, when my father and I had a brief conversation. I asked him how he was—his toe, his back, his shoulder—and he told me in a few short sentences and again handed the phone to my mother. For Father's Day, I mailed him a card and wrote how much I appreciated what he had done for me. But none of that seemed to matter to him, or make a difference. He has returned to passing the phone to my mother after hearing my voice on the other end of the line. For eleven months. So I haven't really spoken to my father since our Christmas argument. I don't think he wants to speak to me. I don't think he has forgotten what I said, nor forgiven me, nor seriously responded to any effort I made to meet him somewhere in the middle, between El Paso and New York, between parent and child, between respect and subservience, in this nether world of the family, between right and wrong.

What is that in between? I don't know. Upon reflection, I don't think what I did was completely wrong. I think my father bears as much responsibility for the argument as I do. For years, I think my father and I had a relationship that was mostly fake. He didn't understand my literary world of ideas, and I had long ago left Ysleta, his orbit, and stopped working on the ceaseless renovation and upkeep of his apartments. I had long ago stopped listening politely to his views on Mexican politics and the Catholic Church, on Pedro Infante and the Golden Age of Mexican movie-making. No more did I nod my head at his criticisms of the bizarre, somewhat corrupt American culture he has adopted in name only. I had ceased to live day-to-day around my parents' kitchen, where my mother still cooks and presents meals to my father, who sits on the same stool against the wall next to our Formica table, pontificating about what is on his mind, urging my mother to sit down before her own food gets cold. I am not part of their lives anymore, yet strangely I remain close to my mother, who reads my books, who exercises with "la Denise Austin," who keeps up with world events, who wants to know about Aaron and Isaac and Laura. My mother, I have discovered, has become an interesting adult I can talk to and seek advice from, still my mother, yet also a contributor to my thoughts and questions preoccupying my adult life. The only topic I can't talk to her about is her Catholicism, what her point of view was when I was a child—faithful, redemptive, mysterious—while mine has shifted to open criticism, revolt and pragmatism. She does know I am at best a lapsed Catholic, and I know she is a devout Catholic. We simply leave it at that. Despite our fundamental disagreement, our relationship still bends and sways like a verdant branch on a tree.

My relationship with my father, however, even prior to our Christmas argument, had deteriorated over the years to an exchange of niceties. Whereas I remember many recent heart-to-heart discussions and disagreements with my mother, I don't remember the last in kind discussion with my father. These conversations, where you know your opponent well, and they know you well, and where the issues involved are what you face today, sear themselves into your consciousness. These discussions teach you about yourself, reveal a new avenue of thinking or introduce you to a way of life not your own, but a life that gains a new validity in your mind. I'm not sure why I kept having these conversations with my mother, but not with my father. My father seemed impatient when I analyzed a topic, or he repeated what he always said, rarely adjusting his position, perhaps tired of answering questions from me or anybody else. As an adult, I grew to dislike the pleasant face he donned like a mask whenever guests arrived in Ysleta over Christmas, his fake smile, his grandiloquent gestures as the perfect host, while my mother rushed to and from the kitchen with *menudo* or tamales for their friends and laughed easily with her guests, not trying to be anybody other than who she was.

I don't think my father was always like that, yet I do remember how he became suddenly more religious after he retired, after they had traveled to Jerusalem and Egypt, after his body was shoved to the forefront of his consciousness. For years he had criticized the Catholic Church too, although never as severely as I did. But in retirement, my father returned to God. I know my mother had been thrilled with this development, yet I remember thinking that fear was his motivation, not genuine faith. Was I too hard on him? Had he changed to become a person I couldn't understand anymore, or had I just become more severe toward him, cognizant of my growing financial and geographic independence, perhaps ready to exact retribution for years of real and imagined offenses? My mother had been as tough on me as my father when I had been a child, yet I have never felt the need to pay her back two- and threefold. Something about my father's gestures, what I perceived as his duplicity or disingenuousness, his dictatorial smugness, this residue of his self that had become bitterness on that velvety red couch, that something incited me to attack him. I blame only myself for what I said and did, yet I responded to him, and what he had become, to his tiredness as a human being, to his not being vibrant and thoughtful and open like my mother, maybe even to his getting old and simply marking time. Perhaps I reacted in anger to the prospect of his death, to watching him give up on life, to witnessing his body give up on him.

I do still love my father. When we return for another Christmas in El Paso in one month, I will try again to find out if he will forgive me, if we can really talk and perhaps create another memory that matters to both of us. I will try again, if he is still there, if the hour is not too late. Yet I don't think people should die before they're dead. I don't think fathers should just sit on velvety red couches and stare at the television and daydream about what once was. I also don't think a son should kill a father before his time. I don't think sons or daughters should cram the disappointments and pain of the unsaid over years into one cold afternoon. I don't think sons should ever be so angry, nor fathers so bitter, about time and relationships and memories and a present that beckons only to the shapeless shadows of the past. I don't think these things, I don't believe them, yet here I stand on this godforsaken ground.

# Chico Lingo Days

(Selected entries from the author's blog, Chico Lingo)

December 21, 2008—An Ysleta Christmas

I ARRIVED IN EL PASO, TEXAS, FOR CHRISTMAS YESTERDAY, TO visit my mother, my brothers and their kids. Laura and my kids have always relished this holiday visit, a trek we have made every year since our marriage. It releases Laura's inner shopper, and for a week before Christmas she pump-primes the economy at El Paso's sprawling malls. Aaron and Isaac love their cousins—they are similar ages—and they have spent the first two days playing New Yorkers against Texans (their version of Cowboys and Indians) and exploring the irrigation canal behind my parents' house.

For the past three years, however, this visit has been an awkward one for me. Three Christmases ago, I argued viciously with my father. The argument was ostensibly over something trivial, but in reality it was over old, deep resentments and the bitterness that can sometimes build between a prideful and headstrong father and a son with the same blood in his veins. For three years, my father would not speak to me when-

139

ever I called from New York. Instead, at the moment he heard my voice, he handed the phone to my mother. For three years, even after I apologized to him for my harsh words, my father did not forgive me. He did not say hello or goodbye whenever I saw him at Christmastime.

I thought about many things during those three years. I thought about the argument, and why it happened, and even wrote an essay about it, "This Wicked Patch of Dust." I thought about how I had hated my father's macho personality as a child, his domineering control over my mother throughout the years, his bad decisions made by fiat. I thought about how I hated my own temper, and why I did not roll my eyes as my brothers did, behind my father's back, but instead confronted an old man and challenged him to a fight. I thought about how my mother agonized over our family's rift, my mother the avid reader, my mother who is relentlessly curious about the world, my mother whom I have always believed deserves to stop sacrificing for others and do more for herself. I thought about my father's deteriorating body, how he cannot walk more than ten feet at a time and depends totally on my mother. He is so weak when throughout his life he was indefatigably strong.

Indeed, my father was a good father. Yes, he was tough and occasionally mean. But he did push us to work hard for our family and for ourselves. At Ysleta High, my father crafted my posters when I ran for Student Council; he fashioned an intricate puppet theater for a play I wrote for an English class; he taught me to maneuver the stick shift and clutch of our Volkswagen Beetle. My father had to compromise in his life, primarily by adopting a country in which he could not speak the language easily, with an accent that still embarrasses him today. Rodolfo Troncoso loved Mexico, but he knew his family would gain a better life in the United States. For a better future, he relinquished his voice. He cannot stand how his beloved hometown of Juárez, which he visited with my mother every week for decades, has descended into an abyss of drug violence in 2008. Their great loss: they have not crossed the border all year.

As Laura, Aaron, Isaac and I arrived in Ysleta yesterday, I expected again to make the best of another awkward Christmas. But my father surprised me. As soon as I stumbled through their orange kitchen door with heavy suitcases in both hands, he stood up shakily from his chair—he can't easily move without his walker anymore—and hugged me. At our Formica kitchen table, we talked for a precious forty-five minutes, exchanging news, before I finished bringing in our luggage. I thought perhaps this was a first-day aberration, a momentary lapse in his anger at his prodigal son. But today, again, my father and I have talked and we have even laughed together. Although we have not yet uttered the words, we have finally forgiven each other for being Troncosos.

## January 12, 2009—Killing Latinos in New York

This week *The New York Times* ran a front-page story on Marcelo Lucero, an Ecuadorean immigrant who was stabbed to death in November by young thugs who shouted anti-immigrant, anti-Hispanic slurs: "Latinos Recall Pattern of Attacks before Killing." The news story was about the long-standing pattern of hate in the Long Island town of Patchogue, a pattern unnoticed by the police. The mayor of Patchogue said the immigration debate painted undocumented immigrants as "animals," as outsiders who are "expendable." Immigrants who have brought life back to Patchogue's Main Street are instead blamed for cutbacks in schools, for crime, for bringing an alien culture and language to New York. One of the youths (all have pleaded not guilty) told authorities he only went out "beaner hopping" once a week.

The mayor's point belies the protestations of anti-immigrant talking heads and political demagogues, that they are targeting only illegal immigrants, not legal immigrants, that they attack "those who break our country's laws," not Latinos in particular. When you obsessively focus on every crime by an undocumented worker, invariably from Mexico, when you wave the flag and accuse immigrants of taking jobs from "real Americans" to exploit economic fears, when you characterize someone who is darker than you and speaks another language as sub-human, the thug on the street with a knife in his hand and hatred in his heart will not ask first to see your Green Card. He will stab you and may not bother to ask questions later. That's the reality. Our hateful environment encourages thoughtless acts.

"It is okay to kill a person who shouldn't be here. It is okay to kill someone who does not speak English. It is okay to kill the kind of person whom my mother and father disparage at the dinner table. It is okay to kill someone whom the red-faced Lou Dobbs vilifies on CNN every night. No one wants that kind of person in the United States. I am doing the country a favor; I'll even have fun while getting rid of this vermin." How long will we allow these poisonous rationalizations to seep into American minds? Shall we wait for more killings of Latinos before we stand up against this hate?

On many levels, the American hypocrisy on illegal immigration is stunning. We profit from undocumented immigrants every day. With cheaper food at our tables. With apartment buildings and houses built by these workers. With nannies who take care of our children. American companies and their 401K retirement plans are richer because of the work of undocumented immigrants: food producers, homebuilders, construction companies, restaurants, bakeries. Perhaps we want to keep these immigrants in their shadowy, defenseless status. "Make money off of them, and kick them in ass, or kick them out when we've finished using them," that seems to be the cruel new American credo.

This hypocrisy on illegal immigration extends beyond "white" America, descendants of English, Irish, German, Jewish and Italian immigrants who secured a foothold in the New World by hook or by crook. Some Latinos who have made it here also want to close the doors to any more newcomers. Some African Americans who claim a privileged minority status don't see why any benefits of the civil rights movement should be granted to those who weren't forced to the New World as slaves.

This has never been, and never will be, a black and white issue. We should ask and argue for a return to working out the complex problem of immigration humanely and rationally. We should decry those who use incendiary rhetoric on immigration to climb atop the backs of the weak, for higher ratings or more votes. We are better than that. Perhaps it is too much to ask of human beings to recognize the poor, new outsider as someone they once were, as someone who their grandfather or grandmother might have been. It is too much to ask, but we should nevertheless keep asking America to have an open mind, lest we forever lose the best traditions of the New World.

February 9, 2009—Michael Phelps and the Violence in Mexico: Connect the Dots

Recently my parents in El Paso, Texas, phoned me and recounted another series of decapitations in Juárez, Mexico, their hometown, a place that has become a no-man's land of murder and mayhem. Drug cartels battle the Mexican government *mano-a-mano*, with thousands dead. Meanwhile, Olympic hero Michael Phelps is pictured inhaling from a bong in South Carolina. Whoopi Goldberg proudly admits, to audience cheers, she has smoked weed and demands we leave

Phelps alone. The Daily Show's Jon Stewart jokes repeatedly about bongs and marijuana, making it oh-so-cool to light up. I wonder if anyone will ever connect the dots.

The United States has one of the highest percentages of pot smokers in the world, and our popular culture winks at drug use and even glorifies it. Meanwhile, marijuana is the most important cash crop for Mexican drug cartels. Mexicans die because of our voracious appetite for drugs. I am waiting for Lou Dobbs to anchor one hundred shows on America's responsibility for the murderous disaster in Mexico; I am waiting for Campbell Brown to do a series on how our red, white and blue practices, like our drug use and gun trafficking, cripple Third World societies. Wealthy America has a bong party, but the poor outside our borders pay for it, in blood. On our direct responsibility for the violence in Mexico, the United States is all bias, all bull.

I have no love for the often corrupt Mexican government. I have no love for a society that seems permanently stratified to engorge the richest of the rich while the best hope for the poor is to cross to *el otro lado*. Indeed, my parents' founding myth, why they left Juárez in the 1950s to become American citizens, is about the lack of economic opportunities in Mexico, the need to pay bosses to win and keep a job, and my mother's still fervent American idealism.

We just finished with an American president who seemed to lack any instinct for self-reflection and adaptation to the circumstances, but did this malady infect much of the country as well? We are culpable for the violence in Mexico. True, we are not decapitating police officers and kidnapping citizens to intimidate the Mexican government. But America's drug use is why this is happening south of our border. We are the prize. Our money is the prize. We want those drugs, and whoever sells those drugs to us wins billions of dollars. What strange mass psychosis allows many in the United States to be *shocked*,

*shocked* about the grisly details in Mexico, while millions of our baby boomers and their children inhale?

Recently, the El Paso City Council took up the issue of whether to encourage a national debate to legalize drug use. Just to debate the issue, not to favor legalization. It was a desperation move, in part because those in Washington, D.C. and New York City do not see, across a flimsy border fence, the war zone Juárez has become. Of course, that stalwart of self-reflection, Lou Dobbs, ridiculed the city council for encouraging drug use. But that knee-jerk response is symptomatic of our delusion: we rarely have meaningful debates that lead to honest self-reflection about the consequences of what we do when it comes to Mexico.

I do not favor legalizing drugs. I do not favor another war on drugs. I do favor being responsible for what I do. I favor fighting to be critically self-reflective, even when my psyche's instinct is to defend and promote itself at all costs. We as a country have probably the most important invisible hand in the violence in Mexico. Yet we don't readily and repeatedly admit it. As long as we don't, we will never come close to any solution. True, we will have great political theater, and we will lead comfortable, self-satisfied lives about how cool we can be, while secretly reveling in *schadenfreude* on Mexico. But the United States will have lost many opportunities to avert a future disaster that will assuredly spill across our borders.

February 23, 2009—Encouraging Kids to Read, Encouraging Kids to Excel

This past week has been a momentous one for our family: our fourteen-year-old son has received letters of acceptance from the best public and private high schools in New York City. This has not happened because we are lucky or because we have lots of money. Our son's hard work and focus, as well our creating an environment at home for learning beyond school, have been keys to Aaron's success. I contrast my son's school application experience with my own. I went to a poor high school on the Mexican-American border in which a majority of the students did not attend college. Yet I was successful in El Paso and later at Harvard and Yale because of similar practices at home. How can we encourage our kids to excel in school? This is what I have learned from my parents, and as a parent.

Read to your children early, and regularly, when your kids can't even walk across the living room floor. Reading to very young children nurtures an emotional bond with books, and with you, a bond they want to recreate as they get older. Laura and I read to both of our sons every night, for about half an hour each, for years. Not surprisingly, both Aaron and Isaac are voracious readers, reading about two or three books a week. We read, they watch us read and we've read with them. We buy books and regularly visit libraries. We limit TV time. All these practices create an environment of reading for recreation, of enthusiastically exploring ideas, of reveling in the magic of storytelling.

Give your children the space and attention to follow their intellectual interests. I loved creating gadgets and traps as a kid in Ysleta, all manner of Rube Goldberg machines. My father allowed me to use his tool shed, experiment with his construction materials and bring back "junk" from the dump, which for me was treasure. He taught me how to manipulate his tools and how to use a LeRoy for drafting when I expressed an interest in his work. Similarly my younger son Isaac loves to discover how things work. We often lug home old computers, monitors and fax machines we find on the street so Isaac can take them apart. Good parenting is about paying attention to what your child is interested in, and giving him or her the space and opportunity to pursue that interest.

Teach your child the value of hard work and limits. This was the mantra I repeated to my kids: "If you do well in school, you have your freedom, your TV time, your time on the computer and with video games. But if you don't finish your homework on time, if you don't do it well, if your teacher calls or emails me about your lack of focus or effort in class, then I will be on you like a rash." Nowadays I rarely have to tell them anything, because we made it a practice to finish homework first, immediately after school, before they turn on the TV, before playdates, before relaxing. It was a work habit that became their habit over time. I do not expect them to be perfect; I just want them to live up to their potential. It is gratifying to see them become young adults, and how they have internalized doing well in school for their benefit, not for mine.

Love your kids, and listen to them carefully. Remember, it is about time with them, and guiding them to become the best person they want to be, and not about money, fancy trips or false accolades. Sometimes I have to coax an issue out of my children. Other times I see an issue—over-scheduling, for example—they are grappling with, but have not yet identified. You sit down and talk to them, not to tell them what to do, but to brainstorm the problem, to offer possible solutions, to get them to resolve the problem in a way that works for them. Just letting them know they are not alone and that they can discuss problems with you is already a victory in your relationship with your child. It is hard work and time-consuming, and I have been humbled repeatedly by the process. But I learn and adapt, and I always keep trying to be a better father.

May 12, 2009—Bertha E. Troncoso

I should have written this on Mother's Day, but I was traveling. I did phone my mother, Bertha E. Troncoso, the E for Estela, on the day. My wife Laura and I did send my mother flowers. My kids, Aaron and Isaac, created cards for Laura, our tradition of preferring handmade drawings to anything store-bought. Our family also ate a delicious brunch at G.W. Tavern in Washington Depot, Connecticut, the GW for George Washington. For a long time, my mother has been my family heroine. Here are snippets of her story.

She was born on a *rancho* near Chihuahua City. Anytime I whined in El Paso about throwing out the trash or hosing down the trash bins, she would remind me of not having shoes until she was ten years old. She had a beloved dog named Sultán and a mother, my *abuelita*, who was tough and often cruel. Doña Lola was a single mother with three children before she married the genial man I would know as my grand-father. She survived the Mexican Revolution, machos in *el rancho* and grinding poverty, so maybe my *abuelita* had reasons for possessing a character made of steel.

My mother's family moved to Juárez when she was a teenager. Bertha Estela was so beautiful that she began to model clothes for local department stores. I have seen many pictures of my mother in her wedding dress. In a close-up my father has enshrined in our living room wall, my mother looks like a Mexican Jane Russell.

As my mother recalls, she met my father at a plaza in Juárez. When they married, she had saved more money than him. My father Rodolfo was a poor student studying agrono-my, and my mother held a steady job as a saleswoman. When my father is feeling nostalgic, he retrieves old newspaper clip-pings of my mother modeling the latest post-war fashions.

I remember my mother being the strictest mom on San Lorenzo Avenue. Doña Bertha, as the neighbors called her, definitely inherited her character from her mother. She never allowed us to play at neighbors' houses; our friends had to play at our house, under her watchful eye. On weekends and after school, we worked until we ached. Polishing furniture. Cleaning up after our dogs. Painting the house. Pulling weeds next to the canal outside our fence! I was appointed head of Sanitation. Our neighborhood, a *colonia* next to the Mexican-American border, had gangs, *Barraca contra Calavera*, and drugs, so in retrospect perhaps my mother had a point. As my friends in New York City have said, I grew up in an "at-risk neighborhood." You gain the drive and discipline to succeed with that beginning by having parents who are tougher than the hard-packed dirt beneath them.

As I grew older, I began to notice how intelligent my mother was, yet how she confined herself to the role of dutiful wife. Mamá still has dozens upon dozens of her friends' phone numbers committed to memory. Once, before I left for Harvard, I tried an experiment with her. I said a friend's name, and she would give me their phone number. We got up to 36 before we stopped. She made thousands of dollars as a relentless Avon lady in Ysleta, enough to buy a sleek Buick station wagon with a tinted moon roof. In high school, that was my preferred ride on hot dates. My mother was and still is a voracious reader of everything from *Selecciones* to the Bible. I buy her a yearly subscription to *The El Paso Times*, which she reads from front to back.

Yet she was happy to first take care of my *abuelitos* when they became infirm and had to live with my parents. My mother fed and bathed them until my grandparents died in an apartment my father built for them in our backyard. Now that my father can shuffle but a few feet without his walker, my mother takes care of him. My parents are the same age, but my father is weak and insular while my mother is indefatigable, funny and quick to ask when my next book will be published.

I don't know how she does it. Bertha Estela could have done anything in the world, but she chose to take care of her family. She chose love and sacrifice over personal accolades and accomplishments. Now you know why she is my heroine. I hope I will always follow in her footsteps.

## August 11, 2009—Reaching Back in History to Stop Thinking

I read an Op-Ed article in yesterday's *Wall Street Journal*, "Our Unconstitutional Census," by John S. Baker and Elliott Stonecipher. The authors reach back to a selective version of the U.S. Constitution to argue illegal aliens should not be counted in the 2010 census, because counting them under-mines the equal representation of certain states and their citi-zens. That is, states with large populations of undocumented workers get apportioned more House members and electoral votes than states without. The current census, as authorized by Congress, counts everybody, legal or illegal.

The authors wrap themselves in the Constitution and even the first 1790 census, which counted all inhabitants, to give legitimacy and authority to their argument: "The census has drifted from its constitutional roots, and the 2010 enu-meration will result in a malapportionment of Congress."

But the authors fail to mention one fact that undermines their argument: the first 1790 census counted slaves. African slaves, who did not get the right to vote until 1870, eighty years after the first census, were counted as three-fifths of a person (enshrined ingloriously in the Constitution). Moreover, south-ern states benefited by having more electoral votes and more representation in Congress per voting citizen, to the loud com-plaints of northern states, for the selfsame eighty years.

The authors of the *Wall Street Journal* article also perform a sleight of hand, probably unnoticed by the casual reader, but certainly noticed by this one. They take the word "inhabi-tants" as the correct mandate of the 1790 census, but instead of mentioning that inhabitants for George Washington and his census included non-voting slaves, the *Wall Street Journal* authors use the Oxford English Dictionary's definition of "inhabitant," as a bona fide member of the State, entitled to its privileges. Did African slaves have all the privileges of the State in 1790? Could they vote? Of course not.

What is important to note is not only how this article reaches back selectively to its version of the Constitution, but how much harsher the current authors are on non-voting inhabitants than were George Washington and other Founding Fathers. Baker and Stonecipher want undocumented workers to count for zero in the 2010 census. At least, and it's not saying much, George Washington wanted each slave to count for three-fifths of a person in the 1790 census. Perhaps the Founding Fathers had some empathy for the downtrodden, or for the businesses dependent on the downtrodden.

Many would persuasively argue that today's undocumented workers are analogous to Washington and Jefferson's slaves. Immigrants work menial jobs, often in agriculture, and suffer violence and discrimination, living outside of society and blamed conveniently for all manner of social ills. African slaves were of course forced to come to America and subjected to brutal, systematic violence. But is there any doubt that if slavery were still legal in the United States that we would be capturing our slaves from the poorest, most vulnerable parts of the Third World, including Latin America? What is the same now as before is the need for American industry and society to prosper, often on the backs of the poorest and most vulnerable, and for these workers to be used to the maximum while keeping them as marginalized as possible. We win; they lose. It's not more complicated than that, but perhaps it's not the kind of reflection in the mirror Americans want to see.

Reaching back to ambiguous and even contradictory standards, such as the Constitution, often seems to bolster certainty and conviction, until one takes a more careful look. This reaching back is the problem. It is done to stop critical thinking and gain acceptance of a viewpoint that may have hidden biases having little to do with that historic standard held so high. Anyone telling you there exists a pure beginning we should return to is asking you to stop thinking, and to march in lockstep behind them. Readers, think and analyze. That is the true measure of a good citizen.

## August 31, 2009—Half-mud, half-dead

It has taken me about a week to recover from our Costa Rica vacation. We arrived at one in the morning on Monday night/Tuesday morning. I woke up with a severe head cold, and my back was in spasms. The zip-lining near the Arenal Volcano was fantastic, but now I was paying the price.

I have always acted differently when I am sick. When I was younger, I ignored any ache or cold, but if my sickness truly debilitated me, I either lashed out at whoever was nearby or I sunk into a temporary depression. This week, barely able to walk, my head, eyes and nose gushy with fluids, I slept. I slept until I couldn't sleep anymore. I kept quiet and observed everyone busy around me, Laura, Aaron and Isaac. I was in a cage, and that cage was my body.

It was a strange experience, my week-long illness. I was feverish, and I wanted to recover. I thought about my father and his chronic back problems, which eventually reduced him to a walker in his mid-70's. I really did not want to become my father. I lay in bed, wincing with pain, not quite able to breathe right. I felt like part of the bed, as if I were sinking into the mattress itself. I imagined I had been abandoned in a mud pile. I was now half-mud.

It's not bad being half-mud. You have no responsibilities. You lie in bed, or mud, and look at everything. Conversations occur around you, about you, but you are not a part of them. A crash in the other room? Somebody else rushes to see what it is, to clean it up. For me, for that week, there was no drive within. That was the fascinating part. No anger. No self-loathing. No urge to do. The kids needed to get ready to go back to school? Their usual pain-in-the-ass father could only glance at them, weakly semi-conscious. "Action Bear" (Laura's oft times moniker for me) was in hibernation. Half-asleep. Delirious.

There was a point, later in the week, when the bed felt too soft, when I stopped thinking about the strange colors in front of my eyes, when I thought about what bills needed to get paid by the end of month. That's when I knew I was better. I missed being half-mud, half-dead, and I even wanted to go back. I imagined for a few hours before I rose like Lazarus from the dead why Lazarus would even want to get up from being dead. I mean, if you could be half-dead, observing the world but nothing else, that would be the ticket.

As I hobbled to the mailbox and to Broadway Farm for pounds and pounds of California yellow peaches, nectarines, Cortland and Gala apples and a watermelon the size and weight of a bowling ball—Do all young teenage boys eat this much fruit?—I missed my half-mud existence. Zabar's. Dry cleaning. The mailbox again. Returning emails. Filling out back-to-school health forms. My back was still killing me. But I could more or less walk now. I explained to Isaac, as he watched me grimace on the sidewalk, "It feels as if a crazy carpenter has driven nails into my spine." But yeah, I was getting better.

By this weekend, I was fully resurrected. My back had but a hint of my previous torture, and what was left of my cold was a weak cough. Gone was the Pumpkin Head of the half-mud man. Did you have the swine flu? somebody asked me. No, I don't think so, I replied. But perhaps for one week I did live the strange and sweet existence of a Pig Man in the Half-Mud.

November 2, 2009—Is the Texas Library Association Excluding Latino Writers?

I had a wonderful time at the Texas Book Festival, which was well-organized and full of lively literary parties. On Saturday, I walked through the white tents next to the state capitol, gathering handouts from commercial publishers, lit organizations and university presses. My panel was not until Sunday, so this was my day to play.

But as I stopped at the Texas Library Association's (TLA) table and perused a yellow handout entitled "2009 Tayshas Annotated Reading List," a book list compiled by public and school librarians from the Young Adult Round Table (YART), I noticed precious few Latino authors or subjects. In fact, as I counted and reread the book summaries (later confirmed by studying the books online at booksellers), only three were by or about Latinos. Three out of 68 young adult books recommended by the TLA.

This fact was disturbing enough, but then I walked to the panel on the Tomás Rivera Children's Book Awards, with Benjamin Saenz (*He Forgot to Say Goodbye*) and Carmen Tafolla (*The Holy Tortilla and a Pot of Beans*), and previous winner Francisco Jiménez. Saenz and Tafolla's award-winning books are aimed at young adults. Both authors are from Texas. Both books are published in the time period covered by the TLA list, 2007-2008. And both books were excluded from the list. Margarita Engle's *The Surrender Tree* (a Newbury Honor book) and Oscar Hijuelos's *Dark Dude* (starred review from Booklist) were also not on the TLA list, and that's after a cursory look at 2008.

As I sat listening to the panelists talk about fighting to have Mexican-American literature included in the canon of American literature, as I heard them talk about their struggles to reach young Latinos with stories that reflect their lives, I admired the careful words of Saenz, Tafolla and Jiménez. But at the same time I seethed at the TLA. What was going on here? The juxtaposition between what the TLA was peddling at their table and the Tomás Rivera panel was jarring.

My anger burst out during conversations at the Texas Book Festival. I asked for explanations. One well-known Texas writer said it was the "morality police" mentality of certain Texas librarians, who enforced their morality more strictly with anything Latino, a sophisticated kind of ethnic discrimination. A Texas librarian said it had to do with the YART panel itself, who was on it, who recommended books, but even she was surprised the TLA list contained only three books by or about Latinos. "That's pathetic," she said.

Indeed, it is. Latinos comprise about half the current students enrolled in Texas K-12 schools. When we or the media decry the high Hispanic high school drop-out rates, are we also training school administrators to be bilingual? Welcoming non-English-speaking parents to become involved in the schooling of their children is essential. I know my mother did not feel, nor was she ever treated, like an alien when she went to talk to my teachers or the principal at South Loop School. Why? They spoke Spanish, even the *güeritos* who were not Latinos. But that was El Paso. What about Houston, east Texas, the Panhandle?

When we complain about low Hispanic high school test scores, are we also providing reading lists that inspire kids throughout their schooling, books that say the stuff of their lives is real literature? The *School Library Journal* said of Carmen Tafolla's book: "This collection will be sought after by both teens and teachers looking for strong characters and an eloquent voice in Chicana literature. While regional appeal will certainly drive purchase of this book, libraries looking to diversify and modernize their story collections will also want to consider adding this worthy title." But apparently not in Texas, if the TLA has any say-so about it.

The issue is not creating an "affirmative action" literary list. That's a great way to put down Latino literature while pretending to help it. We do have high quality literature, by any standard, by national standards, in the Latino community. We have writers who are craftsmen, who are highly educated, who are creating stories that win national awards and sell tens of thousands of copies.

So I am not asking to lower standards and make a new TLA list with 45.6 percent Latino writers. That's ridiculous. But the effort has to be made to look at the new reality in writing and in Latino literature in particular, and to understand that there need not be a sacrifice anymore between diversity and quality. But to do that, we need open minds and their goodwill.

I don't want any librarians (from Texas or anywhere else) angry at me. El Paso public libraries changed my life and opened my mind to writing. For me, Carol Brey-Casiano is an exemplary Texas librarian who *promotes* Latino authors. I just want the Texas Library Association to think about what it's doing, and to consider a better way.

(Note: The TLA list did have three books about girls at "elite boarding schools," and two books on Australian teenagers.)

## November 16, 2009—Latinos and Jews on Hanukah

Laura is traveling for work, and tonight Aaron, Isaac and I lit the candles for the sixth night of Hanukah, the Jewish festival of light. We took turns lighting different candles, and sang the prayers. I knew the first part, but hummed the rest. The kids were my guides. In a few more days, we will be in El Paso. If we attend a Christmas *posada* in Ysleta or midnight mass at Mount Carmel, Laura and the kids will also join me.

How did we become this interfaith, multicultural family? It all began in college, in Economics 10, when I saw this composed, attractive sophomore sitting a few rows in front of me. We chatted a few times that year. She thought I was Greek; I thought she was English. We were both wrong. I was a Chicano from El Paso, Texas, and she was a Jew from Chicago and Concord, Massachusetts.

I really became friends with Laura at a Mexico seminar the next year. Laura was majoring in Government, fluent in Spanish and focusing on Latin America. We jogged together for months along the Charles River before we began dating. If you want to get a sense of our first kiss, read my short story, "Remembering Possibilities," in *The Last Tortilla and Other Stories*. Laura is always embarrassed when I mention this, but it is a moment I wanted to immortalize in my work. That's one of the hazards of living with a writer: parts of your life may end up in the lives of literary characters.

It wasn't always easy being a couple. My parents adored Laura, primarily because she spoke Spanish, but also because she was easygoing, *"suavecita"* and *"muy gente,"* as my parents would say, while I was sometimes stubborn and mean, *"el terco que no se aguanta."* Laura fit better in semi-rural, small-town Ysleta than I ever did. Laura's parents, however, did not like me because I was not a Jew. Sure, their attitudes changed for the better after many years, after they appreciated that I loved their daughter and wasn't going away. I also grew to relish their focus on family and the intellectual debates at the kitchen table. Today, our harmony, mutual respect and, yes, even love are achievements, but they were hard-won.

A few years ago, an engineer with the same last name wrote to me, and sent me a research paper on our surname, which is unusual in Mexico. He had traveled to obscure archives in Mexico, traced the Troncoso name to the same town of my father's family and even traveled to Spain to study the archives of the Catholic Church. His findings? Our surname originates from "Trancoso," and has Sephardic origins in Toledo. "Los judíos de Trancoso" were either cypto-Jews hiding their heritage because of the Spanish Inquisition, or Jews kicked out of Spain to the New World in 1492. I have a book, by Pere Bonnín, *Sangre Judía: Españoles de Ascendencia Hebrea y Antisemitismo Cristiano*, a bestseller in Spain already in its fourth edition. This book compiles research on Spanish Jew-ish ancestry, and my last name is in this book.

As Laura quipped when I told her, "Now I now understand the attraction."

So I may have Sephardic ancestors, but given my mother's fervent, unyielding Catholicism, I probably have Tomás de Torquemada's ancestors, too. Perhaps we became one big, messy *familia* long ago. But I believe Laura is my family, and her family is my family, not because of what happened five hundred years ago, but because I love Laura. I know the qual-ity of the person. That's why I light the Hanukah candles even though Laura is not at home. It is what our family does. It is what I do.

## January 7, 2010—Harold Hernesh

I am late sending out my holiday cards again, but I did remember to slip one under Harold Hernesh's door. Harold lives in our building on the Upper Westside, and our family, including my children, befriended Harold when we rented a one-bedroom across the hall from him. The following year we bought a co-op in the same building, but on another floor; Isaac was a mere three weeks old. For thirteen years, we have lived in this building-qua-miniature-city of 354 apartments on Manhattan's Upper Westside.

Harold, who is eighty-seven years old, always reminded me of my grandmother, Doña Dolores Rivero, a survivor of the Mexican Revolution. Both were tough, gruff and perpetually in mid-scowl. Yet if you stopped to talk to them, and got to know them beyond their flinty exterior and garbled retorts, beyond their complaints about dogs or inept store clerks or greedy banks, these *viejitos* revealed a fearful vulnerability of what they had seen and what they had barely escaped. Harold was eighteen when he was imprisoned by the Nazis at Dachau in 1941, for being a Jew.

I have given Harold copies of my books. He doesn't know it, but I made a version of Harold a hero in my story of violence and redemption, "Remembering Possibilities."

Yesterday Harold stopped me in the lobby and handed me three lollipops, one for me and each of my children. He always carries candy in his pockets and hands it out to children, or their parents, every day. I have a jar of Harold's candies in the kitchen. For years, Harold sat with his sister in the lobby of our building, chatting and introducing her to his friends. But Harold's sister died recently. Harold is now alone.

So when he uncharacteristically asked me to follow him to his apartment, I said yes. I had been to his place before, to fix his cable because he had forgotten he needed to have both the cable box on and the TV on channel 3 for the system to work. Honestly, how do oldsters survive in this complex, idiosyncratic world? I don't know. I struggle with these problems myself, and I can only imagine what shape I'll be in when I'm eighty-seven. Will I be able to manage an apartment by myself at that age? Laura and I can barely do this now.

"The Lithuanians! They were worst than the Nazis!" Harold blurted out as he handed me a book to read, a story of another Holocaust survivor. When Harold says words like "Lithuanians" it sounds like "Lith-punians," and he half-spits every other word he says. It's possible Harold had a stroke a long time ago, but I've never asked him. His blue-gray eyes wandered into the distance. His pale, brown-spotted face reddened. He recounted a story I had never heard before. As he said, "The luk-thpiest daay of mai lifept." The luckiest day of Harold's life.

A Nazi soldier and his Lithuanian collaborators had taken him to a field of mass graves and ordered him to dig. He would be digging not only his own grave, but the graves of other prisoners who would be shot that day. His spade hit the ground, but it was frozen solid. They beat him and yelled at him to dig. Harold smashed the shovel into the ground, but still the ground would not give. They snatched the shovel away from him and tried to dig themselves, to no avail. "The luk-thpiest daay of mai lifept," Harold repeated. On Broadway, bitterly cold and windy days like today, he said, have never bothered him.

I don't talk to Harold, nor did I ever bike fifteen miles as a kid to visit my *abuelita* on Saturdays, because I feel sorry for old people. I listened to them, because I loved their stories. I relished the bittersweet humor that came from hardscrabble or harrowing experiences. They took me there, wherever "there" was, and I was captivated by and transported to another world. For me, it was their gift.

## February 26, 2010—228 Miles

Tonight I drove 228 miles, from Lawrence, Massachusetts, to New York City, through a monsoon for the first 194 miles. After Greenwich, Connecticut, it was a snow hurricane, which at midnight still roars outside my apartment window.

It was the most treacherous driving I have done for a while; I witnessed the aftermath of at least six accidents. On the Merritt Parkway, where on a normal night most ignore the 55-mph speed limit and cruise at 70-plus, every inch of road glistened, the lane lines were invisible, and cars slid and swerved even at 40 mph. For four and a half hours, let's just say, it was tense.

I was in Lawrence this morning to give the Daniel Appleton White Fund Lecture, created in 1852 by Judge White, who was a contemporary of Hawthorne and Emerson. Judge White, whose memoir I discovered through Google Books, was the first president of the Salem Lyceum and an advocate of democratizing knowledge through public lectures and discussions.

In the memoir, I noticed how open-minded he was, and truly far-sighted. Judge White deeply believed in his Protestant faith, yet castigated fellow Protestants who instead of possessing a culture of openness and inquiry were of an "opposite spirit," who "judging, censuring, avoiding and reviling one another," undermined the right of others to be more or even less devout than them. He admired the Puritan immigrants and their search for religious freedom in the New World. In the spirit of Judge White, I talked about how Latinos can develop their voice and become full-fledged participants with cultural and political power in our American experiment.

The trip was worth every treacherous mile. Before the lecture, I conducted a workshop with ESL students at Northern Essex Community College. The stories the students told me about their lives as Dominicanos in Massachusetts, or immigrants from China and Bangladesh, were hilarious and poignant. We talked about how we have often been put down for having accents, or why even family members or neighbors might make fun of our dreams to educate ourselves.

We exchanged stories about how to find the right mentors, how to focus on yourself even when the world is hostile and how to build that sense of self-esteem that keeps you focused on your goals. I took apart their oral stories, and showed them how naturally they were already excellent storytellers who could make an entire room break down with laughter. I pointed out the plot climax they so easily crafted and the true-to-life dialogue they inserted into their stories about encounters with police and immigration officials. The lecture was a great experience, but talking to these students, from twenty to sixty years old, was the highlight of my trip. These students have so much to say, and they do indeed have great teachers in Lawrence helping them say it.

I like an exchange with the audience as much as I like giving a speech to focus on complex points about culture, philosophy or how I survived throughout the years. I learn as much from my audience as I feel they learn from me. These trips, like the trip to Lawrence, energize you and make you believe again that storytelling can make an essential difference in creating a better self, inspiring group self-reflection and building a community from far-flung elements.

## March 31, 2010—The Loss of Juárez

I am back in El Paso with Laura and the kids, having just been in El Paso two weeks ago for the Juntos Art and Literature Festival. The kids have spring break at their schools, and we needed a break from New York City.

We visited the Centennial Museum at UTEP, which was closed for César Chávez Day, but the Chihuahuan Desert Garden, around the museum, was open. We spent a leisurely hour or so marveling at the variety of cacti, giant carpenter bees and yellow-and-black butterflies of the garden. The peace of the garden's nooks, El Fortín and other hideouts amid the flowers and sun refreshed us unlike anything in recent memory.

But as we drove back to Ysleta on the Border Highway, a sense of sadness overtook me. For two years, my kids have been clamoring to go to Mexico. My wife and I have said no, because of the rampant violence in Juárez. Today we settled for stopping on the shoulder of the freeway, just after the Bridge of the Americas and on top of the Yarbrough overpass, for pictures of Mexico and the infamous border fence my children have studied in school.

The violence and the wall have separated us; it is no compensation to look at Juárez from afar. I wish my children could know the Juárez I knew as child. But I will never willingly put them in harm's way.

What others who have not lived on the border may not understand is how close El Paso and Juárez were and are even today. Close culturally. Many with families in both cities. Close in so many ways. When I was in high school in El Paso, my family always—and I mean every Sunday—had a family dinner in Juárez at one of my parents' favorite restaurants: Villa Del Mar, La Fogata, La Central, Tortas Nico and Taquería La Pila. It was going back in time, to the city where my father and mother met and were married. But it was also to experience another set of rules and values, to a mysterious country with more bookstores than I ever saw in El Paso, to *tortas* and open-air *mercados*, to *primos* who would drop everything to show me their horses and even to my first funeral—the open casket is still vivid in my mind. A young boy, the son of a friend of my parents, had been run over by a car. Juárez for me was primal and vivid; it was my history. I thought I understood it instinctually, even spiritually, and that's just when it baffled me the most. After graduating from Harvard, I spent a year in Mexico City to get my fill of this labyrinth of a country.

On Monday just before we came to El Paso, I was trying to explain this to friends in Boston, at a Passover Seder. How El Paso was closer to Juárez than New York City was to New Jersey. How people went to lunch in Juárez and were able to return to the United States in a couple of hours. How we used to go to Waterfil over the Zaragoza International Bridge (on the outskirts of Juárez) for Easter picnics, clinking cases of sodas or groceries we couldn't find in Ysleta. Yes, it was that close, in the most trivial and profound ways, and we took it for granted.

Two years ago that world changed. Two years ago an unprecedented orgy of drug violence exploded in Juárez. Two years ago we lost Juárez, as a place to show our kids where their *abuelitos* came from, and in so many other ways. It is a deeply felt loss for many of us in El Paso.

I am tired of pointing out that the voracious drug habits of the United States and the millions of dollars of American guns illegally exported to Mexico are root causes of the drug violence. Not to mention a corrupt local police force in Mexico, and an ineffective national government. For the moment, the hypocrisy, the idiocy and the cheapness of life are too much to bear.

I just miss Juárez. It was never a joke for me, as it was for some of my Anglo friends and not a few of my Chicano friends from El Paso. It was a portal to another world that felt at once deeply familiar and strangely fascinating. When will this nightmare end?

## June 20, 2010—Illegal Is Illegal

That stupid tautology is what passes nowadays for thinking in today's debate on illegal immigration. It's stupid, because instead of explaining or justifying anything, that tautology glosses over the complex context of undocumented workers in the United States, and how many of us benefit from their work. With such glibness, we wash our hands of understanding their plight.

It's good to be a hypocrite in this country on illegal immigration. It's rare anybody calls you on it; it's rare self-satisfied hypocrites do any reflection. Illegal is illegal. That's it. Case closed. I've even seen that slogan trumpeted on political placards in upstate New York.

I was in Missouri last week, staying at a nice hotel, paid by the school that brings me in to conduct writing workshops. As I was editing and grading stories and essays from my students, there was a knock on the door. Two women with cleaning carts smiled sheepishly as I opened the door, and said in heavily accented English they would come back later.

I beckoned them in, saying it was okay. As I worked, I heard them chat in Spanish about Mexico defeating France in the World Cup. I introduced myself in Spanish, told them my parents were from Chihuahua, and saw their jaws drop. Yes, we were all Mexicanos, the guy in the oxford shirt with the Macbook in front of him, and the ladies who were cleaning the toilets and vacuuming.

I spoke to Julia for a while, from Guerrero. She told me she desperately wanted to learn English, but had no time. *"Traba-jo dos trabajos. Diez y seis horas seguidas, y no me da tiempo."* That is: "I work two jobs. Sixteen hours back to back, and I don't have the time." She smiled a toothy smile while she said this, and my heart wanted to break. I asked her how they treated her at this hotel, and she said the manager was extremely nice to them. Julia told me she sends money back home every month, to her family in Guerrero.

What is remarkable to me is how often this scene has been repeated in about every hotel I have stayed in America. A few months ago, I was in Denver at an annual conference of writers. At one of the fanciest hotels in the Mile High City, again an undocumented worker was cleaning my room. I chatted with María Teresa. As we spoke on the second day, she was almost teary when I handed her a signed copy of my first book, *The Last Tortilla and Other Stories*. I told her to have her children read her the stories. I almost lost it myself when she responded, as we said goodbye at the door's threshold, that she wanted her children to become like me.

These are the people who are the overwhelming majority of the undocumented workers vilified by the idiots in Arizona, and elsewhere, as illegal immigrants. They are the salt of the earth. Many of them are desperate to be *americanos*. But Americans already in power, many of Italian, German, Irish and Scandinavian descent, have forgotten how their grandfathers and great-grandmothers arrived in the New World. We want our hotels clean, and cheaply, so we can profit from the labor of Latin American workers.

We want our strawberries and apples picked beautifully, without bruises, and cheaply. But we turn the other way and somehow don't hear when someone explains how this is possible at high-end markets like Fairway or Zabar's in Manhattan, or across the country at Stop & Shops. Who is in the fields picking our fruit, for hours under the merciless sun? Who cares! Illegal is illegal, they say happily, as they stuff another strawberry in their faces at the Marriott.

I instead talk to undocumented workers, especially if I see them working diligently to make our country better. I ask them how they are. I listen to their stories. And I can only respect them in return. That's the decent thing to do. That's the right thing to do. When did we become so callous?

Again, this week as I walked on Broadway, in front of giant photographs of voluptuous supermodels at a Victoria Secret mega-store, who was rebuilding the sidewalks? With sweaty headbands, ripped-up jeans and dust on their brown faces? Their muscled hands quivered as they worked the jack-hammers and lugged the concrete chunks into dump trucks. Two men from Guanajuato. Undocumented workers. They both shook my hand vigorously, as if they were relieved I wasn't an INS officer.

I imagined how much money Victoria Secret was making off these poor bastards. I wondered why passersby didn't see what was in front of their faces. We use these workers. We profit from them. In the shadows, they work to the bone, for pennies. And it's so easy to blame them for everything and nothing simply because they are powerless, and dark-skinned, and speak with funny accents. Illegal is illegal. It is a phrase, shallow and cruel, that should prompt any decent American to burn with anger.

July 8, 2010—Traveling Alone Together

I am toward the end of Walt Whitman's *Leaves of Grass*, on my iPhone no less, and I have relished every second with this poet. Just as with Emily Dickinson's *Collected Works*, which I also read on my iPhone, I have longed to take a leisurely subway ride, or to have a free hour or so before I sleep, to reenter this portable world of words.

Whitman and Dickinson are so different. I admire Dickinson's almost mathematical precision and rhythm. Her abstractions on poems often match my thinking in an uncanny way: as her song ends I understand, and yet the idea lingers in the air and adds depth where no words are written.

Whitman however unleashes the line from any certainty, and revels in nature's details, as if ideas would only intrude in the world before our eyes. I admire Whitman's enthusiastic camaraderie, his openness to sex, immigrants, the offbeat and the wonder of being alone.

Both poets in a way seem alone with their poetry. They are to me deeply humanistic, yet this is not a humanism that values the chitchat of society, or the glib conclusions of casual and catty observers. They seem alone to me because they travel within themselves. To stop and remark politely would despoil their journey. They hearken to others—what writer does not want to be read?—but these others are those like themselves. They are traveling alone together.

I started Chico Lingo to communicate, debate, chronicle and explore the days before me. At times I write to you, the reader. Sometimes I plead for understanding. On other occasions, yes, I will pontificate and complain. But I also write to myself. It is one of the interesting and peculiar activities human beings can do: they can reflect on what they think, through writing in my case, in which my "thinking" is arranged into words and paragraphs, through Chico Lingo.

I embarked on this journey into myself principally because this is how I have always been. I want to be alone together with others who are not glib, who question what is given to them by authority or tradition, who wonder at thinking and understanding the process and who see what is in between the said, the concluded and the promised. When I have ignored this "searching self with an acute perspective," to give it a name, I ignore myself. I do it when I am in a hurry, when I am in pain and when I am weak-minded. And I have always regretted it later. It is as if I had temporarily lost who I truly am.

I have often imagined it is the soul reaching out, this thinking and writing alone together. This soul is meant to be understood and read, and it is meant to reach someone, but that audience is whoever listens and perhaps is limited to those who already will not forget the quiet self that shadows them even within their family. The audience for this soul, instead of being a target, grants itself into the company of those wanting to be alone together.

So I seek my audience with a vague hope to be heard, but even if I am not, if my words and strange musings remain unread and not understood, I would still reach into the darkness. I don't know why. It is not *for* the audience. Nor is it for a vain self. It is—how can I explain it?—at once to sanctify and upend life, to lift it from what it is, to focus thought into words and create a call to what was and what is when we live.

# Finding our Voice: From Literacy to Literature

I WANT TO THANK NORTHERN ESSEX COMMUNITY COLLEGE and the trustees of the White Fund for inviting me here today. It's a pleasure to visit Lawrence, Massachusetts, an "immigrant city" over hundreds of years, from the English Puritan ancestors of Daniel Appleton White who first settled here in 1640, to the successive waves of Irish, German and Italian immigrants in the nineteenth century and the Jewish immigrants at the turn of twentieth century, to more recently *los dominicanos* and *puertorriqueños* and other Latinos who have become the majority in Lawrence. It is this great American experiment in translation—the translation of the ideas of freedom, democracy, hard work, family, community, tolerance—to successive new groups and new cultures that I want to focus on today.

What has happened in Lawrence, with Latinos becoming the majority and gaining more political, economic and even cultural influence is similar to what I witnessed growing up in El Paso, Texas, a stone's throw from the Mexican-American border. The biggest difference in El Paso was that *mexicanos* have been the majority of the population for at least one hundred years, but only recently, say in the 1970s and 1980s, as Mexican Americans became the majority of registered voters and the Latino business community grew in size and power, did this majority population translate to political and cultural power. The existence of Mexico along the border also changes the dynamic in El Paso: as an American citizen you can truly live in between two languages, two cultures and really, as a part of this hybrid culture called *la frontera*. I believe Lawrence and El Paso are at the forefront of what is happening in America. Latinos have become the largest minority, and the issues before us are how do we translate ourselves, our values, our varied cultures, into the American experiment, and how will our participation in turn change the United States. Latinos have, and will continue, to change. This country will continue to change. Many within our community, and without, will resist this change. But if the United States is about anything, it is about immigrants coming into their own, joining this country as full-fledged citizens and finding their voice.

Let me start by focusing on my experiences as the son of Mexican immigrants, but let me briefly tell you why I do it this way. I believe we learn better from example than from a vague idea to be such-and-such a way. In this manner, I am Aristotelean: I believe you learn and gain knowledge by doing the right thing, not by simply theorizing about what is right. What I do, and what I did, are much more important than what I say. (Somebody please impart that lesson to the would-be Solons of the U. S. Congress.) So an example for me is more powerful as a moral guide than an exhortation or admonition. That's why I write stories: if I can make the reader believe in and care for a character in one of my stories, I feel I am more likely to change that reader's life, to illuminate it with a new look at an old question, than by simply writing an abstract treatise. Not surprisingly, moral character is the groundwork of Aristotle's ethics.

The second reason I focus on my experiences is because I don't think I am remarkable in any way. I believe many of you, if not most, can do a better job than I did of educating yourself, of focusing on your family, of contributing to your community. When I arrived at Harvard, I was terrified and begged to go home. When I saw my first book on a bookshelf at a Barnes and Noble in New York, I had a weird out-of-body experience: someone, an impostor, had used my name, written about my neighborhood in Ysleta and El Paso and was cashing checks for my stories. That couldn't be me, could it? In my head, I often still think of myself as the stubborn, fat little boy everybody ignored. So yes, I know you can do better than I ever did. You can take the journey I have started, further down the road. My example, I hope, will be a challenge to you, and a call to action.

How did I get to be who I am today? Judge White, in his instructions for creating this series of lectures on August 23, 1852, said he wanted them "to enlighten the mind and elevate the character of the young of both sexes...with a deep conviction of the importance of early cultivating those virtues, habits and principles which constitute excellent character and furnish the most reliable resources for their advancement and success in life." Don't be too surprised when you discover how much an admirer of the Puritans and a contemporary of Hawthorne and Emerson has in common with today's Latino immigrants.

My father and mother, Rodolfo and Bertha Troncoso, both from Juárez, Mexico, came to El Paso in the 1950s, as newlyweds and new American residents. They did not have any money, and in fact we lived with my *abuelita*, Doña Dolores Rivero, in El Segundo Barrio near downtown El Paso while my parents built their adobe house in Ysleta, a *colonia* without electricity or running water. I remember that as children we started living on San Lorenzo Avenue in Ysleta when the house was still unfinished, with square holes instead of windows, exposed copper pipes and wiring and a spooky outhouse in a backyard overlooking an irrigation canal. Acres of empty lots surrounded us, horse and cattle farms, dusty, unpaved streets and at night, a desert darkness absolute except for the palpitating lights of the Milky Way. Loosely knit street gangs also gathered around midnight bonfires near the banks of the irrigation canals. We had a hard life, but I do not think my parents ever became cynical or self-defeatist. In fact, the more setbacks we had, the harder they tried, the harder they worked and the harder they made their children work.

My parents still live in that same house, and it is the house I stay in whenever I return to El Paso. Eventually they did trade in their Green Cards for passports of the United States. Recently they celebrated their 50th wedding anniversary. But more importantly, this is what my father and mother have accomplished: all four of their children not only graduated from college, but also have graduate degrees. And yes, my father and mother were, and are, *mexicanos* who speak primarily Spanish. How did they accomplish this?

The first and most important gift my parents gave us was unconditional love, but this was not I-love-and-justify-everything-you-do, but I-love-you-no-matter-what-you-do-and-I-expect-you-to-do-what-is-right. Unconditional love with the highest expectations for moral behavior, for self-respect, for being good to others. And yes, if we made a mistake, we would correct it ourselves, and make it right. We would always be responsible for our own behavior when it fell short, and they would not rescue us. Unconditional love with self-responsibility.

The second lesson my parents taught us was the lesson of self-discipline about your work. The love of hard work, not because you love to work, but because you love the work you do. When we were young, my parents put us to work around the house, pulling weeds, polishing the furniture, painting the house, carrying bricks and sacks of cement, even cleaning the canal behind our house, because they did not want us to get into trouble in Ysleta. We were a family, and they expected us to work together for everybody's benefit. But as my sister and my brothers and I grew older, my parents adapted. My father and mother understood school, and its activities, were becoming more important. They did not tell us what to study in high school or what activities to pursue; those would be our choices. But whatever we did choose, we were expected to work hard for success. In fact, the only way to escape knocking down another wall and hauling the pile of rubble to the dump was to have homework, or a school project. Menial work or mental work? The answer was obvious to me. Why do you think I became editor-in-chief of the school newspaper at Ysleta High?

The final important lesson my parents taught us was that they had time for us. Time to help us with our projects. Time, and a selflessness, to consider and support what we wanted to do. Since my father and mother did not speak English very well, and since they were working hard simply to survive, they usually did not help me with my homework. But that did not mean they did not become involved in my school, or my school projects. Instead of feeling embarrassed about their accent in English and completely excluding themselves from my school—an understandable, but I still think, self-absorbed attitude—they did what they could. At every open house at South Loop School, my mother went to see our school projects and to talk to the teachers, however she could. Most teachers and administrators knew Spanish, so that was helpful, and I am sure that essential fact embedded my grade school into our neighborhood. When my mother asked questions, or volunteered to watch the playground with other mothers, she was not demeaned as if she were an intruder or an alien. I remember she baked cupcakes for our school trips and attended dozens of car washes; my mother also handed me money every month to buy paperbacks from the Scholastic Book Club. My father, a self-taught engineer, built a two-story cardboard house with me, for a puppet show I gave one day in school, painting the façade, creating the puppets and their characters, making doors and windows that actually opened and closed. I also remember my father and mother making posters with me when I ran for Sophomore Class President in high school. So you see, they got involved in their children's lives. They did not give up simply because they did not know the language very well. They found other ways to help. They found the time to care often about things they did not completely understand. And I have never forgotten that. How do we teach parents to reach beyond themselves, beyond their limitations and obstacles, to give their children a better chance for success? I am not sure I know exactly how to do this—it's about having good judgment as a parent, patience and practicality and perseverance—but I know it can be done.

So when I talk about translating the best parts of Latino culture to foment success in America, I am focusing on nurturing the character in children to work hard to succeed, even in a tough environment like Ysleta. These moral (dare I say Puritan) lessons are not extraneous to the Mexican-American community. As I have said before, my parents were, and are, *mexicanos* through and through. And there existed other *familias* in our neighborhood of Barraca that began with nothing but a patch of dirt, and their children became teachers, lawyers, doctors and librarians. Of course, there were also families who wasted time and lacked discipline, who succumbed to drugs or other methods of self-destruction or who valued immediate menial work at the price of long-term education and success. But the good examples were, and are, right there in Ysleta, right here in Lawrence, within the Latino community. We must never forget that and sell ourselves short. The challenge to academic theoreticians and government officials is to find out and honestly understand why the culture of some families allows them to take one, two, twenty steps forward toward eventual success, or at least a higher probability of success, and why others are left behind. But Culture, with a capital C, is not easily quantifiable, so it runs against the culture of the academy. And Culture is also complex, so it will never be captured by a politician's glib sound bite, nor will it be easily altered by well-intentioned, but far-removed bureaucrats. So it is left to the rest of us, parents, teachers and, yes, writers, to find how and why good character is nurtured within our community and how to encourage it. Unconditional love, with high expectations and self-responsibility. The discipline and focus of hard work, with the freedom to choose and to determine yourself. Finally, time with your children, with the adaptability to work through or around obstacles. These three lessons from my family, for me, were the groundwork of my literacy. I cannot say it any simpler than this: To change this world, we must begin at home.

As I grew up in Ysleta, reading and libraries became the focal points of my life. What is the role of libraries in encouraging Latino children to read and write better, and yes, to learn about themselves and their heritage?

After I amassed a huge collection of comic books, adventure books, mysteries and history books with the money my mother gave me for the Scholastic Book Club, I suddenly realized, just before high school, that I did not have to own a book to read it. I could borrow it from the library. As an adult, I still have not completely broken that habit (maybe I never will), and I still buy an enormous quantity of books. Every room in our apartment in New York City has shelves full of books, books piled in corners, books on chairs, books on the bed. A story and a new world in every corner. There is something special about owning books, even if they are only small paperbacks, as most of my books were in Ysleta. Not only can you lose yourself again, and reread a good story and remember the details you have forgotten, but read books become a catalog of your mind in way, a mental history of where you have been and what you have experienced.

Since the libraries at South Loop and Ysleta High were closed on weekends and during the summer, and since I wanted to find a library I could borrow books from, I decided to travel to the downtown public library when I was thirteen years old. I do not remember why I did not try the branch library in Ysleta, which of course would have made more sense. But I do remember that my older sister, Diana, who was already a senior in high school, told me about the main branch of the El Paso Public Library. On my first trip, she drove me to the library in our battered lime green Volkswagen, and helped me get a library card. Later she even took me to the People's Emporium across the street on Oregon, to smell the incense and stare at the weird gifts and knickknacks in that store. But as a thirteen-year-old, I did not want to depend on my older sister. I needed to find a way to get there myself.

So I began a strange, but wonderful odyssey to the El Paso Public Library on many Saturday mornings. I would check the tires of my old three-speed yellow bike, and strap on a portable radio to the handlebars. From my mother, I would borrow a pouch to carry water, candy bars and if I was lucky a bag of Cornuts. We did not have fancy water bottles custom-made for bicycles yet, nor shock-resistant bike radios. I warned *mis padres* when I was ready to start my voyage. They would remind me to take extra dimes to call along the way, to be

careful and to avoid the speeding cars and dangerous intersec-
tions. My mother would make the sign of the cross over my
face and chest before I jumped on my bike. Then I would start
my fifteen-mile trip from San Lorenzo Avenue, usually before
eight in the morning to avoid the afternoon heat, and bike
west on Alameda, one stoplight and dusty corner after another, to downtown El Segundo Barrio. To visit my *abuelita*. For
an afternoon at the El Paso Public Library.

I nearly died a few times. Once, I was racing across a street
corner on Paisano, and I half-slid underneath a city bus that
suddenly crossed my path. My front wheel was crushed, but
the bus missed my body by a few inches. I never told my parents about that little incident. I also had other nasty scrapes
and falls. But I loved it. Loved the freedom of my bike. Loved
stopping wherever I wanted to stop. Loved listening to my
favorite rock songs on the radio. For me, these bike trips down
Alameda defined a glorious El Paso summer.

When I arrived at my *abuelitos'* house on Olive Street,
right across from the Consulado Mexicano and the old offices
of *El Fronterizo* newspaper, Doña Dolores and Don José wel-
comed me with hot Mexican chocolate and *bizcochos*. My
*abuelito* often drove me in his rusty green-and-white Chevy
station wagon to the Western Auto on Paisano when I needed new parts for my dilapidated bike. But the best part was sitting on their front porch and listening to stories about the
Mexican Revolution and living on *el rancho* near Chihuahua.
At night, her cigarette and coffee cup in hand, Doña Dolores
recounted the days when Francisco Villa rode into town and
strung up a few cowardly politicians or greedy bankers on
street lamps. Once in a while, with a gleam in her eyes, my
grandmother cranked up her rickety turntable and twirled my
grandfather to the heavy beat of Mexican polkas.

From my *abuelita*'s, usually in the afternoon after I had a
chance to recover from my long trip, I would bike to the main

branch of the El Paso Public Library. I found books about Villa, Obregón and Zapata, stories by Mark Twain and S. E. Hinton. I first read Rudolfo Anaya at the El Paso Public Library. I discovered, when it was too hot, that I could walk downstairs and read in the cool library basement, which was supposedly haunted. I wandered into the Southwest Room, which seemed fancy and forbidden. I sometimes sat next to the newspaper section and the big window overlooking Oregon, where the splash of sunlight made me feel warm and safe. For every mood, for every story, there was a perfect corner in the El Paso Public Library, and I relished my time there.

In retrospect, one main reason any public library is important is because it is free. It levels the playing field a bit. Even if you have no money, you can go there to explore ideas, to read about other times and cultures, to think. Yes, the El Paso Public Library gave me access to more books, but it also gave me access to a culture of sitting down quietly to read, without disturbance. The library provided me not only with free books, but free space, both of which were invaluable. I suppose I could have found a quiet place in my house, and sometimes I did. But there was no guarantee that it would remain so. At home, I would also be tempted simply to watch TV or play with my dogs. But in the library, not only did I read more, but I read more carefully and deeply, because I could stay there until my mind was exhausted. In many ways, those early years prepared me for the strenuous and extended concentration I would need for my studies in the Ivy League. I exercised my mental muscles in the library, and lo and behold, I transformed myself from a casual reader into a focused one. So it was more than just free books, but also free space and a culture that reinforced settling down, deep reading, thinking, imagining and exploring with my mind. I am no doubt a writer today because I had a place to go as a kid, where I knew stories were essential and where everybody also reveled in the wonder within books.

Of course, now as a father, I have tried to instill my love of libraries and reading in my two sons, Aaron and Isaac. When the children were in grade school, every two weeks my wife Laura and I would take them to the St. Agnes branch of the New York Public Library for "Library Day." The kids each chose about 5 to 10 books to read during the following two weeks, sometimes with the help of a librarian. At home, we also attempted to nurture a culture of reading. Aaron, when he was nine years old, would routinely get up at six in the morning and read for two hours before school started. He finished about two to three novels per week. Isaac, as a seven-year-old, would sit quietly with his favorite books about collecting rocks and shells, or would meticulously study science books for children and attempt the experiments in the bathroom! And yes, my children watched TV, but I limited their TV time to about one hour per day. One day an administrator at their school took me aside and asked me: "How do we bottle what you are doing? How did you turn your kids into such great readers?" Here are a few lessons I have often shared with other parents.

First, read to your children every day, and start early, when they are one or two years old. When our children were toddlers, we typically read to them at bedtime because reading together was, and is, an intimate and quiet time for our family. Laura read to one of the boys, and I read to the other, and then we switched. As Aaron began to read novels by himself, I sat next to him and asked him what he liked and did not like about the book. In fourth grade, he did a report on Hernán Cortés and the conquest of the Aztec Empire. I was amazed at the level of detail Aaron retained, and how he could organize it after reading several books. So once your child starts reading on his own, you have to take the time to engage him in whatever interests him, and listen and ask questions.

Second, at the beginning, read slowly, point to each word and never force your children to read or write if they are not ready. It is important not only that you read to your children every day, but how you do it. Before my kids turned two, Laura and I taught them not just their letters but also the sounds the letters make. Phonics. We also read whole words and sentences in books for beginners. The makeup of syllables. The rhythm of words. The singsong of rhymes. I also spoke Spanish often, so they would understand the sounds, and become at least orally bilingual. When Aaron and Isaac began to understand words, to look at the text I was pointing to instead of the colorful pictures, I lingered over each word, allowed them to digest words slowly. I encouraged them to create other words by dropping or adding a letter. I tried to make it a game, and I certainly never had the intention of making them into super-scholars. I only wanted to share my love of words and stories with them.

Finally, make reading and storytelling a part of your family's culture. When I took the boys to school in the morning, or over the dinner table, I recounted stories about Lobo or Princey, my dogs in Ysleta, or I encouraged them to make up their own stories. Children naturally love stories and have powerful imaginations. Words and stories should become things they use and manipulate like clay. Before, and sometimes after, we saw the "Harry Potter" movies, or "Holes," "Cheaper By The Dozen" and "October Sky," we read the books and talked about how movies were often derived from books. We also had chapter books about "Arthur" and "SpongeBob Square Pants" for Isaac in second grade, to connect what he saw on the TV with the written story. Many times my children told me that the books were much better than what they saw on the silver screen.

So I do not think it takes magic to turn your children into good early readers, and enthusiastic long-term learners. It takes time with your children, even when a million other tasks demand your attention. It takes patience and warmth, even when you are dead-tired and have not slept more than five hours the night before. It takes curiosity about the words on a coffee cup, the words on street signs, the world of words around you. It takes appreciation for the stories from your *abuelita* as well as stories from other worlds and other languages and even other media. You can help your children first to decipher these words, if you only take a careful look. You can help them to string these words together into a story, if you take the time.

It is not necessarily only about money, although it is true we need to support our public libraries enthusiastically. It is about utilizing free resources, and taking time with your children, and in the right way. It is about caring enough to make the effort to help your children, and then being smart enough to adapt not only to overcome obstacles but also to meet their changing needs. Good judgment about education, as Aristotle understood, will only be appreciated with good practice.

I am proudly a product of El Paso public schools: South Loop and Ysleta High. As an adult and as a writer, I have returned to my alma maters many times, not only because I am loyal to them and because I feel a good sense of obligation to my community, but also because I want to see firsthand what has changed, and what has not. My family has also kept me in touch with the current issues at El Paso schools: my brother, Oscar, is principal of Anthony High School, and my other brother, Rudy, is an English teacher at El Dorado High School.

First as a child in Ysleta, and then as a teenager, I understood very well who were, and who were not, the good teachers at our schools. Not only did I get a lot of information from my older siblings, who already had many of the teachers I eventually had, but I started to appreciate the good teachers, and why they were good teachers. I still remember brief conversations I had with Mrs. Laurie Ryan as a child, and some of her lessons to our fourth-grade class. Our questions were discussed, not dismissed. We were looked straight in the eye while she stopped what she was doing. She corrected our mistakes while still being encouraging. I remember Mrs. Dolores Vega, in third grade, and how she danced *cumbias* in the classroom and taught me to be proud of my Mexican heritage. Many of Mrs. Vega's lessons were not part of the curriculum, but they became part of my heart. I also remember Mr. Preston Smith, my math teacher in eighth grade, and how cool and confident he was about my ability in math, when I certainly was not. Mr. Smith half-encouraged half-pushed me into Number Sense, the math club. When I won three gold medals in citywide competition, this fat and shy little boy finally started believing in himself. I also remember Mrs. Juwanna Newman, who introduced me to poetry and rewriting what I thought was perfect prose, and who possessed an infectious love for words. All of these teachers cared beyond the requirements of their job, and they were certainly not jaded in any way, nor did they teach by rote. They engaged the student, they adapted to the circumstance and individual while maintaining high standards, and they taught by experience, by making problems or issues relevant to the lives of students, by allowing the students to learn by doing.

Probably the most influential teacher I had was Pearl Crouch, the newspaper and yearbook advisor at Ysleta High School. Mrs. Crouch was not an easy teacher, and in fact, she reminded me a lot of my *abuelita*: tough, direct and adamant about the good she expected from me. I had plenty of teachers who were tough because they were mean or probably tired of their work, but Mrs. Crouch was tough because she cared. She was not only hard on me and my newspaper writing, but she was hard on everybody. When another teacher attempted to censor my newspaper articles, Mrs. Crouch exploded. She marched into the principal's office, and vehemently and successfully defended me. As long as I was telling the truth, however harsh, as long as I had the facts on my side, she would not let my adult detractors touch me. Sophomore and junior year, Mrs. Crouch took me to San Francisco and New York City, to compete in high school writing competitions. I still remember how we attended my first Broadway show, "A Chorus Line," and how we had dinner at Sardi's, the famous restaurant in Times Square. She opened my eyes to a bigger world, and I will never forget that. The summer of my junior year, at her urging, I applied for and won a scholarship to attend the Blairstown Summer School for Journalism in New Jersey. Only two were selected from the state of Texas. This experience of living away from home and taking care of myself, of being immersed in a rigorous academic environment for six weeks, was pivotal to easing my transition from high school to college, when I went to Harvard the following year. So I do owe a lot to Mrs. Crouch, and all the good teachers I had in El Paso. I have learned their lessons of commitment to work, patience with children, incessant enthusiasm and curiosity, intellectual toughness and independence and sacrifice for others.

Despite the string of good teachers I had growing up in El Paso, I would change a few things in El Paso schools, if I could. The most obvious to me is how little is taught about the history of El Paso and Juárez in the classroom, particularly the history of Mexico. I know that El Paso is part of Texas, but it is also obvious that El Paso's history is inextricably linked to Mexico. Did you know that both Victoriano Huerta and Pascual Orozco, two major figures of the Mexican Revolution, are buried in El Paso? When I went to college, I studied Mexican history and politics and economics for four years, because in Cambridge I realized I knew next to nothing about where I came from, where my parents came from and how El Paso has been, for centuries, an essential crossroad to our bi-national and bi-cultural history. I know we get our textbooks from Austin, but I am not from Austin. We should adapt to the realities in El Paso. We should not devalue what we have in our local communities by ignoring our history, because in the long run we only end up devaluing ourselves, and this place we call home. The White Fund's effort to bring Latino authors to Lawrence, Massachusetts, is a great example of a positive adaptation to a changing local community.

In El Paso high schools, I also learned precious little about the literature of Mexican Americans. It seems obvious to me, and to many educators, that to appeal to a young reader or potential writer that you might start with a story that is relevant to that person's life. That does not mean Latino students should be exposed to only stories written by and about Latinos. I have learned from Chekhov and Faulkner as much as from Anaya. But there should, indeed, be significant exposure to good Latino literature for students from El Paso, Texas, to Lawrence, Massachusetts. And let me emphasize that adjective "good," and in so doing, make another point clear: there is no compromise in literary quality, or at least there need not be. Excellently crafted stories now exist by and about Latinos, stories perfect for middle schools, high schools and colleges, in part because our literary community has exploded in numbers, has matured in focus and has raised its standards through self-criticism. So there is no excuse, anymore, for these lapses in our schools and libraries, except a lack of goodwill, or a lack of effort, or a lack of knowledge about what is available today.

When I arrived at Harvard at eighteen, also the alma mater of Judge White, I did not feel I belonged. I was surprised to learn how few students from across the United States were bilingual.

Didn't everybody relish the brilliant wordplay of the Mexican comic Cantinflas? New friend after new friend also commented on how "cute" or "weird" or "exotic" my accent was. I had an accent? In my battered luggage, I possessed only dozens of T-shirts, from Led Zeppelin to Carlsbad Caverns, and blue jeans. New England got cold? I was terrified at how sophisticated everybody else seemed, at how easily my fellow freshmen could chat with a Harvard professor after class while I scurried out of the lecture hall. For the first time in my life, I was brown against a white background. I just wanted to survive.

I was an outsider in Ysleta, a bookworm in a neighborhood with gangs, and I was also an outsider at Harvard and in the Northeast. Instead of getting drunk on weekends with my friends in my freshman dorm at Hollis Hall, I lost myself in the splendid corners of solitude within Widener and Lamont libraries. Why? First I did not want to disappoint my parents. I knew they were sacrificing themselves financially to send me to Harvard, and I knew they were proud of me. I didn't want to let them down. So this sense of community responsibility, I think, is a good one: to measure up to the good standards set by your parents, and to fight to achieve those standards. But that wasn't the reason I *mainly* avoided the bacchanalia of Harvard undergraduate life. The more important reason was that I believed I could do it; I believed in myself. I had an internal sense of self-worth, in part encouraged by my father and mother, but also by my community. I lost count how many times I heard at Harvard and later at Yale that I did not "act like a minority." What exactly did this mean? That I was not subservient? That I did not assume I was inferior? That I was not drowning in a vicious vortex of self-hate? In El Paso, Latinos and specifically Mexican Americans were and have been the majority for decades. But it was more than that. My parents not only expected me to be proud of my heritage, but they demanded I be responsible for my actions. "Not acting like a

minority" meant for them not just to assume my rights as a citizen, but to embrace hard work, self-reliance and honesty,
however uncomfortable it was for me. Although I was initial-
ly besieged at Harvard, I knew who I was. That's how I was
able to fight this new battle.

At Harvard, I discovered two professors who changed my
life: Terry Karl and John Womack. Professor Karl taught me
about Latin America, but more importantly, she showed me
how to be enthusiastic and committed and precise about my
work. John Womack, an Oklahoman in cowboy boots who
was a powerhouse professor at Harvard, reminded me of home
and taught me about academic integrity and social justice and
Mexican history. Professor Karl, by the end of my junior year,
had agreed to be my thesis advisor. Senior year, when I
enrolled in a seminar on Mexican history with John Womack,
I wrote a paper on modern trends in the workers' movement
(with research I had completed the summer of my junior year
in Mexico City). After I turned in the paper, Professor Womack wrote that I had written the best paper he had read for
that seminar in five years. Those words meant so much to me,
meant I belonged, meant I had somehow found my place at
Harvard despite often feeling in exile in the Northeast.

In Cambridge, my character of being *terco, enojado* and
*orgulloso* (stubborn, angry and proud) also served me well. I
finished my senior thesis, and received two stellar grades for it,
and a third grade that was okay, not great. The title of my first
opus? "Petrolization and Regime Disconsolidation in Mexico:
A Narrowing of Options for Development." What can I say? I
was a cocky Harvard undergraduate trying to solve the world's
problems in my head. I studied Latin American history and
politics, because in Texas I had learned nothing about where I
was from. I also needed to survive the academic hothouse of
Harvard. I relied on one great advantage I possessed: I could
read and conduct research in Spanish. Yes, I was surviving,

even thriving, in college, but I did not like what I had become: a self-absorbed undergraduate who was only too ready to focus on making money and gaining more power.

The third, somewhat dissatisfied reader had written, "This thesis, although original, is obviously written by someone whose native language is not English." In the solitude of my dorm room at Quincy House, I hated myself and my political-science prose for not being Shakespearean. I hated myself for being a law-school-or-bust Gov major, when I really wanted to write stories. I hated the gap between my El Paso English and the Hemingway and Faulkner I devoured in the library stacks. I did not yet posses what I wanted: a literary voice. I hated the visceral pull of "success" that in my mind permeated every nook and cranny at Harvard. I hated that reader.

That reader, an assistant professor, summoned me to his office before my thesis was sent to another reader for an additional opinion. He assured me he would probably recommend a more favorable final grade, but he wanted to discuss the original research I had conducted in Mexico City the summer before. This research was not yet available in the United States. Casually, the professor mentioned he had used documents and statistics cited and compiled in my thesis in an article *he* was writing. He showed me a draft of the article. It did not mention my name, a lowly undergraduate, but it did mention the documents and statistics in my thesis and how I had analyzed them. Could he please have copies of these documents? he asked me. I said I would happily give him copies, but my research was in Texas, at my parents' house. (I lied; it's good to know how to lie at Harvard.) I could send him the copies after graduation. He smiled, and told me not to worry about my grade. I never sent him copies of my research. I hated him too, and all that he stood for. This was one of the many lessons I learned at Harvard.

What did this culture from my family, reading and libraries, and these teachers and schools eventually accomplish? They provided me with an education. But this word "education" means more than what you learn in school. "Education" to me means finding your own voice, and having the ability to accomplish your dreams, and producing your own opportunities to realize the work that defines you as a human being. My education gave me the skills and focus and discipline to write literature. I was able to traverse the chasm from literacy to literature. That was my road to success. For others, their education may not lead them to writing short stories or novels, but maybe they will find their voices as great engineers, path-breaking doctors or astute lawyers. Maybe others, with their education, will discover meaningful work as teachers or artists. But the point is that education means the freedom to define yourself in the world. The freedom to be successful in your chosen field. Education, finally, is power.

So as you struggle to get educated, in school and beyond, remember that you are readying yourself to leave your mark on the world. This precious opportunity, the opportunity and promise of an educated life, should be seized with gusto. You should readily sacrifice every bit of energy to ensure that this opportunity continues within you, beyond your school exams or the exhortations of your teachers. Because once education becomes part of your character, then you become a self-propelled human being, a lover of questions and a relentless seeker of answers. You will be on your way to achieving what Aristotle might call the full potential of a human being.

I believe my primary role as a writer and lecturer is to help educate myself and others. I want to bring people back to thinking, back to reading, back to taking the time to consider the many complex possibilities in an excellent story. A good writer should ask the reader to take a minute, and then take an hour, and then perhaps more than that, several days, to immerse the reader in a story that brings forth complex characters, not caricatures, difficult problems which may not have easy solutions, if they have solutions at all. A good writer should be able to communicate to the reader, "I know your life. I know what you have truly experienced. It's not right or wrong. It's survival. It's making mistakes, and trying to redeem yourself. It's imperfections, and trying to make yourself better. It's outrages, and crimes, and insults, which often are not righted, which you have to fix yourself, in your own mind, in your own heart, so that you are not poisoned." All these things, and more, a writer should do for a reader.

In a good story that reaches the reader, a new world of characters dawns, characters who may not be like you, but yes, you understand them, you want to know what happens to them, and when they are hurt, physically or emotionally, you as a reader are hurt too. A good writer teaches a reader this empathy—but not by beating you over the head and saying, "Believe in this protagonist, or else!"—but by finding what is common between reader and character, and by encouraging the reader to think, and truly participate in making a story come alive. Is it at all surprising that throughout the centuries different dictators have ended up burning books to stop this quiet revolution of empathy?

Like Judge Daniel A. White, I am also a lover of books. In his memoir,[1] which quotes from his letters and journals, Judge White writes about not only possessing thousands of books, in one of the great private libraries of Massachusetts by the time of his death in 1861, but also about giving away thousands of books to family and friends. He writes about books expanding his mind, being "dear friends" and encouraging him to experience what he had not known or understood before. This cul-

---

[1] Daniel Appleton White, *Memoir of Daniel Appleton White*, prepared agreeably to a resolution of the Massachusetts Historical Society by Rev. James Walker, D. D., Boston: John Wilson and Son, 5 Water Street, 1863.

ture of openness and inquiry, not only led him to establish the White Fund to democratize knowledge in lectures and public forums, but also informed his Protestant faith. Judge White criticized those of an "opposite spirit" who "judging, censuring, avoiding and reviling one another" undermined the right of others to be more, or even less, devout than them. We should be no less open and tolerant than Judge White.

How do we as Latinos find our political and cultural voice in America? We find it by being self-disciplined and self-reliant. We find it by adapting ourselves, just as my parents did, to the English language, to a culture that expects you to stand up to be heard. We find it by responding to, instead of ignoring, the false caricatures of Latinos portrayed by those fearful of change, by those who do not want to share power with a rising minority. We find our voice by reaching out to others. While some slam the door in our faces, others will help us. They will be the ones who embrace the spirit of Judge White to be exacting and honest with oneself, while being open to strangers and their new worlds. We find our voice by taking the stones and arrows flung our way, real and imagined, and binding our wounds, and responding so that by word and deed everyone will know we will never give up. Finally, we find our voice by teaching, by believing we are vehicles to help others, all others, but in particular those nearby, our children, our neighbors. We help them by teaching them what we know, and by listening for what they can teach us to become better human beings. Thank you.

The White Fund was established in 1852 by Judge Daniel Appleton White, a contemporary of Hawthorne and Emerson. He was a member of the Massachusetts legislature from 1810 to 1815, was elected judge of probate of Essex county, Massachusetts, an office he held for thirty-eight years. He was a member of the Essex Institute, to which he donated 8,000 volumes, and of the Massachusetts Historical Society. Judge White was the first president of the Salem Lyceum. In previous years, the White Fund has brought such speakers as Horace Greeley, Frederick Douglas and Phillips Brooks to Lawrence, MA.

Sergio Troncoso gave the White Fund Lecture on February 25, 2010.

# Why Should Latinos Write their Own Stories?

WHY SHOULD LATINOS WRITE THEIR OWN STORIES? WHY SHOULD I write stories about Ysleta and El Paso, Texas? The first and probably most important answer to this question is that we write stories about our community to preserve our heritage. But we should also write stories that challenge this beloved heritage. I think we should be proud of who we are, but we should also be self-critical and reflective about what we might want to be in the future.

Most importantly, we write stories about our community to preserve our heritage. The very first story I wrote, for example, "The Abuelita," is really the most autobiographical story in *The Last Tortilla and Other Stories*. It is really a story about my *abuelita*, my grandmother, and the ferocious drive and spirit she had when she was alive. When I wrote this story, I wanted more than anything else for others to know my beloved *abuelita* and to understand what she meant when she said: *El que adelante no ve, atrás se queda.* She, more than anyone else, gave me the strength and courage to fight for my dreams. I think I also inherited much of her don't-bullshit-me attitude. Doña Dolores Rivero. She was in many ways my heroine. I wanted to keep her alive in my story. I also wanted to share her with the world.

In other stories, I also wanted to portray the strength of our *familias* in Ysleta, the love that we have for each other, and even the conflicts that can lead to a better understanding and appreciation of each other. In the story "The Snake," Tuyi, the fat boy everybody ignored, is a seventh-grader at South Loop School. Tuyi is in many ways an outsider in school and on San Lorenzo Avenue where he lives. Yet his *mamá* and his *papá* do not ever forget to show their son that they love him, that they are proud of him. Tuyi may be fat. Tuyi may fart a lot. Tuyi may not be the greatest athlete in P.E. But he is loved. And that love propels him to accomplishments that eventually astonish his neighborhood.

So in many different ways, we can write stories to preserve the memory of our *familias* and to remember our old neighborhood. We will always belong in this family and in this place in a way that we will never belong with anyone or anywhere else. It is our duty to preserve this heritage and to affirm it and even to celebrate it by writing stories about where we belong. We have a great culture right here on the Mexican-American border. We have a great heritage in Ysleta and El Paso. There is no need to look somewhere else for approval or for higher standards. We have strong families here. Our people are tied to the land. We are for the most part direct and honest. It is true that there are some *cabrones* here and there. But we are not yet lost in the world. We still do have more civility than hostility toward a stranger. Most of us still believe in something holy. And let me tell you, that is not the case in many places outside of Ysleta and El Paso. In too many places. Sometimes it takes leaving El Paso for a while to appreciate what we do have here.

So when you are seeing these hundreds of miles of empty desert between you and the rest of the world, you should not feel isolated or out of touch. You should feel lucky.

I said that many of us write stories to preserve our heritage. I certainly do. But that is also not the only thing I do when I write my stories about Ysleta and El Paso. I do not write autobiography. I do not write history. I write fiction, and I like to explore different possibilities and ideas. So although my stories may often have the familiar backdrop of San Lorenzo Avenue or Ysleta High School, they are also explorations into the variability of human consciousness. My stories are sometimes explorations into the unknown or even into the controversial.

In "The Abuelita," while I was portraying my grandmother, I also wanted to explore how an older person might face the final years of her life, how she might face her own death. I wanted to explore a reconciliation with death that was practical, instead of abstract, and that valued the everyday wonder of life. That's how my *abuelita* faced those final days. She always wanted to taste the *asaderos* from Licon's Dairy just one more time. And in "The Gardener," I wanted to explore how two older persons, who are separated by race and class, can make a bridge toward one another. Maggie Johnson and Don Chechepe can build that bridge because the passage of time has given them the perspective that, out here in the desert, we do have more things in common than we don't. I may say "hola" and you may prefer "howdy," but we are both greeting each other and trying to make a connection at the bottom of this prehistoric sea.

I know that we often have problems between the classes and the races in Ysleta and El Paso. Simply because I write *fiction* does not mean I do not have my eyes open to the harsher realities that do exist. The door has been slammed in my face too, even as a graduate of Harvard and Yale. I will tell you a story about something that really happened to me a couple of years ago. I was visiting my parents, and I was walking along San Lorenzo Avenue, the street in Ysleta where I was born. And I was stopped by the *migra*. There was only one guy in the pale green truck. He gunned his motor and stopped his vehicle in front of me to prevent me from going anywhere. He asked me for identification, and I told him that I was an American citizen and that I was just walking around my neighborhood. I was a little angry. "Was it illegal not to have a car in Ysleta?" I asked. "Was I suspicious simply because I like to take long walks?" I told him that I would show him nothing and to leave me alone. I walked away. He muttered a few expletives and spat out his chewing tobacco. I heard him drive away a few seconds later.

I know what you are thinking. But you're wrong. That *migra* guy wasn't a *güero* with a cowboy hat. He was a Mexican American, just like me. So the reality of life can get more complicated than the stereotypical stories we often want to believe. As a writer, I try not only to portray the harsh conflicts we sometimes have with each other, but also the complexity of those conflicts. I really don't want to make the world of my stories too easy for you, or too easy for me.

"Day of the Dead" is one of my favorite stories in *The Last Tortilla*, but it is also a story with a hard edge. Again, I wrote this story not just to describe Juárez and El Paso, but also to lead the reader into a sometimes uncomfortable, but I hope illuminating, exploration. Lupe Pérez is a maid from Juárez who crosses the river every day to work for a well-to-do family in El Paso. She works damn hard every day. She lives a terribly poor life. She sleeps on a foam mattress on the floor. Yet she also has dreams. Lupe is the kind of person we might see every day, but whom we might ignore. She is easily forgotten and dismissed, even in death, unless we force ourselves not to close our eyes.

We dehumanize ourselves when we don't take a good hard look around us, when we forget people like Lupe Pérez. We cannot save the world. I know I can't save it. I will be lucky if I can save myself from having a cold heart. I will be lucky if I can keep my eyes from simply skipping over the unpleasant, the wretched, this person who might seem, at first glance, from an alien world. Yes, I will not exaggerate the terrible of the world like some news shows that seem to select stories with the motto, "If it bleeds it leads." But I will also try to challenge myself, and my community, to look and think about things that our busy world too easily ignores.

In the title story of my collection, "The Last Tortilla," I also wanted to focus on the wonderful heritage we have in Ysleta, our *familias*, but I also wanted to give this focus a twist. The Márquez family in "The Last Tortilla" has lost its vital center of being. The mother has died in a tragic accident, and she has been replaced by another, a *madrastra*, who is hated by the children. *Nuestras mamás* are so important to us. They will always be at the center of our being. But sometimes we take them for granted. Sometimes we do not appreciate how much of the world of security and love and hope they create by what they do for us every day. The good mother. *La luz de nuestra vida.* I wanted to remove the mother from the Márquez family and play out the slow and painful disintegration of this blessed world we all-too-often take for granted.

In this story, I took away the mother to see, for example, how selfishness can start taking over your world when the selfless individual, the ideal mother, is not there anymore. Alejandra Márquez, the oldest child who is thirty years old, finds it much easier to leave the family and get her own apartment now that her mother is gone. Yes, Alejandra still feels responsible for Juanito, the youngest one, and she tries to be a surrogate mother for a while, to no avail. But her sense of "family responsibility" is slowly withering away. And the little boy

Juanito, of course, misses his mother terribly. He sees her in his dreams. He imagines that he is responsible for provoking God to kill his mother. God, for him, becomes a vengeful and punitive figure. Juanito's view of the world, of course, has radically changed because of a tragedy whose secret cause is also an act of selfishness. So this story, "The Last Tortilla," is in part a warning never to forget our good mothers. We should appreciate and love *nuestras mamás* while they are here, and we should never forget the often unseen, but heroic, role they play in our lives every day.

In other stories, I have tried to portray the moral character of our people. Often, we are portrayed as physical and visual beings without a mental life. This is not just a problem of American Latinos being stereotyped, but also a problem of the Hollywood and TV world we live in. This is a world of the visual portrayal of simple desires, not of describing the difficult and sometimes ambiguous choices that form character. When is the last time you saw a movie or a TV show that gave you a sense of the inner worth of a person, of the thinking behind that person's choices? This Hollywood world is certainly not very good at portraying true moral dilemmas. It is not very good at portraying your mental life.

Another story, "A Rock Trying to Be a Stone," is a story not only about three children playing a dangerous game, but also about character. When we are judging someone's character, appearances can truly be deceiving. Turi, Joe and Fernández, three boys playing in a ditch behind San Lorenzo Avenue, have tied up a retarded friend of theirs, Chuy, and have taken him "prisoner." Joe is the older boy. He smokes pot and carries a knife in his pocket. Turi's mother calls him a *cholo* and warns Turi to stay away from Joe. But Turi likes Joe and respects him and knows that Joe is not manipulative. Fernández, on the other hand, is not honest and direct like Joe. Fernández is always trying to fit in and will do everything the easy way if he can get away with it. Although he looks like Turi and Turi's mother approves of him, Fernández has no center of being, really. When their game of prisoners takes an unexpected and awful turn, it is Joe the *cholo* who acts bravely and attempts to save Chuy. But it is also Joe the *cholo* who gets blamed for what happened. So appearances can be deceiving, but all-too-often we make judgments about a person's real character by how they look. Growing up in Ysleta, in the barrio that is still called Barraca, I knew plenty of good characters who might at first glance look menacing and dangerous. If you didn't talk to them, if you didn't try to understand them, then you might lose out on some good, honest friendships.

In conclusion, I want to focus again on a few of the main points I have tried to make when answering the question: Why should Latinos write their own stories? We should write these stories, first and foremost, to celebrate our culture and to communicate our culture to others. I have received mail from as far away as Brazil and Egypt from readers who have found my stories on the Internet. They tell me that they have better understood the Mexican-American culture of Ysleta and El Paso. How distinctive it is. How truly multicultural it is. These readers have also told me that they can understand some of the struggles that we face and how we uniquely contribute to what an *americano* really is. Others have pointed out how they are also seeking answers to these universal questions of self-identity and self-worth, answers to questions about the loneliness of old age and what makes up a family. So as writers of these stories about our *frontera*, we should have that first duty of explaining who we are, in our own words. We should not let others define who we are. We should define ourselves.

I think a great, underlying part of defining ourselves through our stories is having the confidence to do so. I believe we have reached a point where those of us who belong to this culture of *la frontera* in Ysleta and El Paso are not content to sit back and watch others tell us who we are. We know who we are, and we ourselves can tell others about what we love and what we fear and what we hate and what can save us. I believe our community has developed that confidence to step forward and start taking responsibility for the many images that are projected in the name of Ysleta and El Paso. And I said confidence, not arrogance. This confidence means we know we can tell our own stories now, and it also means we accept the burden of this responsibility. It means we keep an open mind. It means we accept the many varied voices of our people. I am simply one of those voices, and I know that.

So in answering my question at the beginning, we should tell our stories so that we define ourselves. The second part of my answer to that question is that we should tell our stories to challenge ourselves. It is easy to sit back and appreciate how unique we are. It is much harder to ask what we should be, and why. We should celebrate our multicultural heritage, but then we should be confident enough about ourselves to ask critical questions about this selfsame heritage. It is not a mark of disrespect or irreverence or cultural betrayal to ask these questions. It is a mark of our cultural strength that we can improve ourselves through criticism.

When I was at Ysleta High School, I wrote for the school newspaper, the *Pow Wow*, and I was a pain in the ass. I had been writing these critical articles about how a certain important student organization, which shall remain nameless, was being run in a shoddy manner. It was simply the truth, and I thought that by writing about it I would get this organization to shape up. Well, soon after my newspaper stories appeared in the *Pow Wow*, the faculty advisor of this organization, who shall also remain nameless, stopped me in the hallway, his face contorted with anger, and yelled: "Sergio, who do you think you are! You should act more like a student! Just wait until I talk to your advisors!" Of course, to their great credit, Pearl

Crouch and Josefina Kinard, my journalism advisors at the *Pow Wow*, never told me to change a word in my news stories. They knew I was right. The facts were on my side. Later, another teacher, who was friendlier to me, said: "Sergio, you give them hell. You keep giving them hell even if they yell at you. Show them that a *mexicano* can beat them with his mind!" I have never forgotten these words. And I will never forget them.